art / shop / eat

Barcelona

D0734137

Lucie Hayes

ten things to do

[1] Climb through Gaudí's unfinished Sagrada Família church (*see p. 99*), but leave time for his other main creations: Park Güell (*see p. 112*), La Pedrera (Casa Milà; *see p. 107*), Casa Batlló (*see p. 104*), and Palau Güell (*see p. 30*).

[2] Marvel at Hotel Espanya (*see p. 37*), Lluís Domènech i Montaner's *Modernista* masterpiece. From the Ramon Casas mermaid mural to sculptor Eusebio Arnau's marble mantelpiece in the breakfast room, every detail is a work of art.

[3] Discover a serene corner of Barcelona at the 14th-century Monestir de Pedralbes convent (*see p. 111*), with its orange tree-filled cloister and painted murals by medieval Catalan artist Ferrer Bassa.

[4] Explore the Boqueria market (*pictured right, and see p. 28*) halfway down the Rambla, an exciting uproar of colours and aromas all assembled to produce one of the city's main events: Mediterranean cuisine.

[5] Impress your family and friends with beautiful hand-made gifts from the host of craft shops at Poble Espanyol complex (see p. 136) at Montjuïc park.

a/s/e Barcelona

[6] Stroll along the beach from the Port Olímpic (*see p. 86*) and Frank Gehry's shimmering goldfish, past the Barceloneta beaches, beyond the fish auction in the port on Moll dels Pescadors, and out to the *Rompeolas* (breakwater) stretching out into the Mediterranean.

[7] Before you wander down the Rambla (*see p. 25*), drink from the Font de les Canaletes (*pictured left*) to ensure a return visit to Barcelona.

[8] Walk through Carrer d'en Carabassa (*map p. 49, G2*). One of the Gothic quarter's most picturesque alleys where little bridges cross over the street, *sgraffito* designs decorate the walls, and the giant figure of Our Lady of Mercy looms atop her basilica at the end of the street.

[9] Unpack your lab coat and research the finer points of molecular gastronomy at some of the most scientific of restaurants in Europe: Alkimia; Cincs Sentits; and Manairó (*see p. 116*).

[10] Stop off at the Fossar de les Moreres (Graveyard of the Mulberry Trees), next to Santa Maria del Mar church (*see p. 78*), a low obelisk commemorating the defenders of Barcelona who fell in the siege that ended the War of the Spanish Succession on 11th September 1714, Catalonia's National Day.

contents

About this guide

The city of Barcelona has been divided into five districts and the aim of this guide book is to enable you to have a great day out in any one of them. For each district first a short selection of the major **art** sights is given, then some other things to see **in the area**, followed by some ideas on the **eat** opportunities—from seafood to seeking out the best tapas—rounded off with our shortlist of **shop** recommendations.

In the **practicalities** section that follows we set the scene with a brief introduction to Barcelona, how to get around, its food and drink, and where to stay. The **history** pages give an overview of the key events in this city's life, while at the back of the book there is a **glossary** covering some of the art terms and key personalities that appear in this guide, as well as a comprehensive **index** to help you find what you are looking for.

Maps are found throughout the guide. Inside the front cover is a map of all Barcelona, clearly indicating where the detailed maps to each district are to be found at the beginning of their sections. The numbers (**1**) on the maps locate the cafés and restaurants described later in that section, and the letters (**A**) locate the shops.

Enjoy Barcelona and do not hesitate to contact us with any views, recommendations or corrections: **www.artshopeat.com**

practicalities

INTRODUCTION

Barcelona is at once a steamy and passionate southern European port
city, a vibrant artistic cauldron and source of avant-garde painters
and sculptors, and an architecture sampler attesting to over 2,000
years of civilization. Defensive walls and classical columns trace
Rome's tenure here between the 1st century BC and the 5th-century
AD Visigothic invasion. Gothic churches, hospitals and shipyards
evoke Barcelona's medieval glory as a Mediterranean sea power,
while 19th-century *Modernista* architecture, much of it by the iconic
and iconoclastic Antoni Gaudí, fills the post-1860 Eixample district.
Today, contemporary stars such as Jean Nouvel, Norman Foster and
Santiago Calatrava push skyward as the city expands up and down
its Mediterranean edge. Barcelona is a forward motion machine that
has always challenged not only its past but its present as well, con-
tinually redefining and reinventing itself with an eye to the future.

Many cities in one—Barri Gòtic, Barceloneta, Eixample—Barcelona
offers miles of beaches, a lively and colourful waterfront quarter
filled with seafood restaurants, art collections ranging from
Romanesque to Art Nouveau to Cubism, and music venues from the
Liceu opera house to the *Modernista* flagship Palau de la Música
Catalana. Throw in a fleet of designer hotels, stylish shops, and
restaurants obsessed with molecular gastronomy and conceptual
surprise, and the result is an early 21st-century metropolis bursting
with energy and creativity. Despite all this cultural and commercial
frenzy, Barcelona remains an easygoing, visitor-friendly city. Mostly
Catalan, part Spanish, part cosmopolitan hybrid, this Mediterranean
crossroads has, in the last decade, taken its place among Europe's
most exciting cities.

PUBLIC TRANSPORT

Getting in from the airport

From Barcelona's El Prat airport, a **taxi** to the centre of town takes about 20mins. The **airport bus** leaves every 12mins from 6am–1am for central Barcelona (Plaça Catalunya; *map p. 22, B4*) in about 30mins. From Plaça Catalunya bus, metro or taxi can get you to your hotel quickly and inexpensively. At night there is a bus (N17) which runs every 20mins from the airport to Plaça Catalunya. The **airport train** runs every 20mins from 6am–10.30pm from El Prat to Sants Station (*see map on inside cover*) and on to de França station (*map p. 74, B3*). The only drawback is the 200m hike, albeit most via a moving walkway, across an elevated passage.

Getting Around

Barcelona's **metro** system quickly, cheaply and safely solves all transport around town (except Sunday to Thursday after midnight), running until 2am on Friday and all night on Saturday, Christmas Eve, and New Year's Eve. City **buses** run daily 5.30am–11.30pm. Lines with red bands stop at central locations such as Plaça Catalunya (*map p. 22, B4*) or Plaça Universitat (*map p. 22, A3*), while a blue band denotes a night bus. **Tickets** can be bought individually at metro stations or the airport but the most economical option if you are staying for a few days is to buy the 'T10 ticket' which is valid for 10 combined trips on buses, the metro and the airport train within a 75-minute period. **Taxi** stands are found near many hotels, at the head of the Rambla (map p. 22, C4), and in Plaça Sant Jaume (*map p. 49, E2*). Radio Taxis can be called on 93 300 1100 or 93 303 3033. Barcelona taxis are usually reliable and fairly priced. If you are staying in the city, don't rent a **car** unless you need one for a day trip outside of town—hotel parking and parking in the city centre are both expensive, and traffic jams are all too frequent.

VISITOR INFORMATION

A very useful website in English to help plan your trip to Barcelona is www.barcelonaturisme.com run by the city's Tourism Bureau, with up-to-date information on the major sites and helpful links. Barcelona Turisme tourist offices can be found at the airport as well as at busy tourist points in the city such as Plaça Catalunya (*map p. 22, B4*); on the Rambla (*map p. 22,C4–23, G3*); and in the Casa Ciutat in the Gothic quarter (*map p. 49, F2*). Multilingual staff are available if you telephone: 807 117 222 (within Spain) or +34 932 853 834 (from abroad).

ENTERTAINMENT

La Guía del Ocio magazine (www.guiadelociobcn.com) lists musical events, restaurants, nightlife, cinema and the main cultural events of the week. Most of the information is in Spanish, but the essentials such as hours and phone numbers are decipherable without major

Entertainment from times gone by at the Liceu opera house

difficulty. *Metropolitan* (www.barcelona-metropolitan.com) is a free English-language monthly publication. Restaurant reviews by Tara Stevens and the general food writing is first-rate.

The leading Spanish-language newspapers, *El País* and *La Vanguardia Española* carry listings for many free cultural events.

SHOPS

Catalonia's textile tradition has always made the city a merchant's paradise, but now that Barcelona is nipping at the heels of Milan as a fashion capital, designer stores are proliferating. Boutiques and shops in the Eixample (*map p. 96, C1–97, D8*) have learned that closing at the traditional Spanish siesta hour (1–5) is bad for business and they now remain open, though many smaller shops in the Gothic quarter (*map p. 49, E2–F3*) still close at midday. Supermarkets are open all day 9–9. The open-air produce markets such as La Boqueria on the Rambla (*see p. 28*) slow down around 3 and close by late afternoon.

The Barceloneta market (*map p. 74, C3*), the Galvany market in Sant Gervasi (*map p. 96, A1*), and Gràcia's two markets, Mercat de la Llibertat (*map p. 96, B3*) and Abaceria Central market (*map p. 96, B4*) are among the best.

FOOD & DRINK
Catalan cuisine

Franco's 1975 demise and the subsequent restoration of democracy brought a late 20th-century cultural renaissance to Catalonia, and the celebration of this reunion with Catalan identity has fervently embraced cuisine. For centuries Barcelona was under the political and cultural thumb of Madrid, and true Catalan cooking became a rural phenomenon. Now all that has changed: Barcelona has rediscovered its gastronomic heritage and brought it back to town.

Catalonia has a fortunate diet: seafood, vegetables, olive oil, garlic and red wine–the so-called Mediterranean diet–have become an international fashion and health statement, and Catalonia is well-placed to make the most of this. The combination of the sea, a fertile hinterland, and the lush Pyrenees to provide dairy produce, game and wild mushrooms also means that the fresh products readily available are more varied than in other parts of the Iberian Peninsula. Catalonia's patchwork heritage also contributes to this variety, pro-ducing a culinary style that has been influenced by Moorish cooking from the Balearic Islands (seen in subtle combinations of sweet and savoury, such as *espinacs a la catalana*, spinach cooked with garlic, raisins and pine nuts); by Italy, which in medieval times was closer by water than Madrid was by land; and by nearby France (the Catalans love a good sauce).

Traditional Catalan dishes include *escudella* (a thick vegetable and sausage stew with pasta, often with chicken added), *esqueixada* (raw cod with peppers and onions), and *escalivada*, peppers roasted over wood coals. Look for combinations such as *cigrons amb xipirons* (chick-peas with baby squid) or *ànec amb peres* (duck with pears). *Botifarra amb mongetes* (sausage and white beans) is a traditional favourite. *Pa amb tomàquet*, bread drizzled with olive oil and tomato squeezings, is a Catalan speciality reminiscent of the Italian bruschetta. Using fish, vegetables, rabbit, duck, lamb, game and ingredients from

9

a/s/e Barcelona

the Pyrenees or the Mediterranean, local chefs frequently produce the *mar i muntanya* (surf 'n' turf, literally 'sea and mountain') combinations of seafood with inland products—*mandonguilles amb sèpia* (meatballs and cuttlefish), for example. Classic Catalan desserts are *crema catalana* (a rich egg custard with a caramelised sugar topping you need to break like ice) and *mel i mató* (honey on fresh cheese).

Catalan wines

The Penedès winegrowing region south-west of Barcelona, with its *méthode champenoise* sparkling wine (cava), has held Catalonia's viticultural centre stage ever since Josep Raventós, owner of Codorníu, uncorked the first bottle in 1872. Though the phylloxera louse decimated Catalan winemaking soon after, the industry refused to die altogether. Presently, there are ten Denominations of Origin in Catalonia: Empordà-Costa Brava, Pla de Bages and Alella (north of Barcelona); Costers del Segre to the west; the Penedès; and Conca de Barberà, Tarragona, Priorat, Terra Alta and Montsant to the south.

Traditional grape types such as Parellada, Garnatxa, Ull de Llebre (Tempranillo), Xarel.lo, Macabeu and Cariñena have been joined by noble varieties including Chardonnay, Merlot, Cabernet Sauvignon and Pinot Noir. Exciting new wines are emerging from Priorat, Costers del Segre, and Empordà-Costa Brava, while the cava industry grows daily. Most Catalan cava is still produced in the Penedès, with giants Codorníu and Freixenet joined by smaller, often better, names such as Agustí Torelló (especially his amphora-shaped Kripta Brut Nature), Gran Caus, Albet i Noya, Lacrima Baccus, Gramona III Lustros and Juvé & Camps. Distinguished non-cava wines from the Penedès begin with the Can Rafols dels Caus winery, with their aromatic reds, whites and rosés. Albet i Noya, Cellers Puig Roca's Augustus wines, the Colet reds, and the Miguel Torres Gran Viña Sol Chardonnay, Coronas Tempranillo, and Gran Coronas Cabernet Sauvignon are other top selections.

The ancient Priorat is now one of Spain's most exciting wine stories. From the 5th to the 11th centuries, when the region's booming Roman wine industry had been abandoned by non-wine-drinking Visigoths and, later, Moors, it was only the Bacchic monks of the Catalan uplands who managed to keep any vines alive at all. Their

legacy lives on, with winemakers such as Álvaro Palacios vinifying powerful, fruity reds—Finca Dofí, L'Ermita, and Les Terrasses—using old Garnatxa, Cabernet Sauvignon and Cariñena vines in the shaly, *licorel.la* soil once cultivated by the Carthusian monks of Scala Dei. Other leading Priorats include Clos Mogador, an intense, complex, inky red wine fragrant with dark fruits; Clos de L'Obac, a simpler, finer brew; or the powerful, full-bodied Morlanda Crianza.

La Vinya del Senyor winebar, typical of many in Barcelona, selling the best of Catalonian and Spanish wines

Other leading wineries in Catalonia include the Costers del Segre Raimat wines (Tempranillo, Pinot Noir and Cabernet Sauvignon) and the Castell del Remei reds and whites. In the Empordà-Costa Brava DO, Celler Oliver Conti is an ascendant star, with the Oliver Conti Negre 1998 (Cabernet Sauvignon, Merlot, Cabernet Franc) rated one of the top red wines in Catalonia, and the Oliver Conti Blanc 2000 (Gewürztraminer, Sauvignon Blanc) a regular on wine lists in Barcelona's top gourmet restaurants.

Recommended **restaurants** are given in each section of this book. Our favourite restaurants carry the Blue Guides Recommended sign: ▬ (see www.blueguides.com for more details). Categories are based on a price per person for dinner, with wine:

€€€€	€100+
€€€	€50–€100
€€	€30–€50
€	under €30

WHERE TO STAY

Barcelona accommodation ranges from luxury mansions to simple pensions. Hotels in the Gothic quarter (*map p. 49*) place you in the very centre of city life, within walking distance to the big sites. Upper Barcelona (*map p. 96–97*) is leafier and quieter, cooler in summer, and offers a break from the helter-skelter of the centre. Hotels in the Eixample (*map p. 96, C1–97, D8*), are conveniently close to shops and the main *Modernista* architecture sites, but the traffic and big-city din are more intense. A full listing of accommodation is available from Barcelona Turisme at Plaça Catalunya 17-s (*map p. 22, B4*) or from its website: www.barcelonaturisme.com.

In this section you will find only a selection of the accommodation available in Barcelona. Hotels that are very good (in terms of location, charm, value for money) carry the Blue Guides Recommended sign: ■ (see www.blueguides.com for more details). The prices below are a guideline only for a double room in high season:

€€€   €300+
€€   €200–€300
€   under €200

€€€ Hotel Arts. Carrer *Marina 19, Tel: 932 211 000, www.hotelartsbarcelona.com, 86 rooms, Metro: Ciutadella-Vila Olímpica. Map p. 74, C4.* This Ritz-Carlton skyscraper may be slightly estranged from city life, parked as it is over the Malibu-like Olympic Port and a 20-minute hike from the El Born neighbourhood, but the place offers a wide range of compensations. Beginning with the permanent mint and ice water on tap in the lobby and continuing through to artworks by the likes of Eduardo Chillida and Antoni Tàpies—not to mention the Frank Gehry goldfish out front—the Arts is an exciting base camp. Sergio Arola's restaurant is one of Barcelona's finest; the Six Senses Spa on the top two (42nd and 43rd) floors has three-hour tag team massage sessions and glass-walled saunas overlooking the Mediterranean, while the general hotel vibe is solid glitz and glamour. Corner rooms on the south façade offer views of Barcelona as well as out to sea and the Collserola hills.

€€€ **Casa Fuster**. *Passeig de Gràcia 132, Tel: 932 553 000, www.hotelcasafuster.com, 97 rooms, Metro: Diagonal. Map p. 96, B3.* This monumental hotel at the bottom of the former village of Gràcia, designed in 1908 (finished in 1911) by Palau de la Música architect Lluís Domènech i Montaner, is an example of the beginnings of a more sobre *Noucentisme* style that followed the *Modernista* movement. Despite the semi-classical exterior, rooms and public spaces have Gaudí-designed chairs, *trencadís* floors and curving door handles, as well as Art Nouveau-inspired lamps. The hotel restaurant serves excellent Mediterranean cuisine, while the lavishly decorated Vienna Café, a historic meeting place for Barcelona's bourgeoisie during the early 20th century, has once again become a popular place for tea or a late *copa*.

€€€ **Hotel Claris**. ◼ *Pau Claris 150, Tel: 934 876 262, www.derbyhotels.es, 120 rooms, Metro: Passeig de Gràcia (Aragó exit). Map p. 96, D4.* This stately Eixample townhouse, Palau Vedruna, now has transparent elevators flying up and down through hanging vegetation and falling water in a brilliant juxtaposition of traditional and post-modern design. The duplex suites are the hotel's most interesting and comfortable rooms, while the rooftop terrace, complete with bar, breakfast area and pool is an ideal refuge in the summer. A block from roaring Passeig de Gràcia, the Claris is surrounded by the city's main shops and is walking distance from important *Modernista* architecture. East 47, the Claris restaurant, is making a name for itself with chef Daniel Padró's original and eclectic interpretations of new and old recipes.

€€€ **Grand Hotel Central**. ◼ *Via Laietana 30, Tel: 932 957 900, www.grandhotelcentral.com, 147 rooms, Metro: Jaume 1. Map p. 49, E3.* In what was once a Cambó family house, a stone's throw from the cathedral and a step or two from Santa Caterina Market, this relatively recent addition to Barcelona's hotel scene successfully combines contemporary design and traditional comfort. The roof terrace (*pictured overleaf*), along with a pool, offers unobstructed panoramas over the Gothic quarter. Rooms are impeccably comfortable. The hotel restaurant, Actual, supervised by star

Views over the Gothic quarter from the rooftop terrace of Grand Hotel Central

chef Ramón Freixa, serves cuisine creative enough to satisfy your curiosity about molecular gastronomy (*see p. 116*).

€€ Hotel Casa Camper. *Carrer Elisabets 11, Tel: 933 426 280, www.casacamper.com, 25 rooms, Metro: Catalunya. Map p. 22, C3.* Charming Carrer Elisabets winds off the Rambla past leafy squares and under towering palms toward the Richard Meier-designed Museum of Contemporary Art. Casa Camper, (of Camper footwear fame) offers a uniquely green lodging alternative: recycled plumbing waters, 100% smoke-free, no tips, free 24-hour snack bar, children under 12 stay for free, and next door to Foodball, where natural ingredients are served in tennis-ball-sized chunks of perfect health, fair trade and sustainability. Junior suites overlooking Carrer Elisabets and the old Casa de la Misericòrdia across the street are the best for getting a sense of the neighbourhood.

€€ Hotel Colón. *Avenida Catedral 7, Tel: 933 011 404, www.hotelcolon.es. 145 rooms, Metro: Jaume 1. Map p. 48, D3.* There is a distinct clubby atmosphere to this elegant Barcelona standby, surprising for a hotel this large. The location is definitely part of its cachet, directly across the square from the cathedral, overlooking weekend

a/s/e Barcelona

sardana dancing, Thursday antiques markets, and, of course, the floodlit cathedral by night. Rooms are comfortable and traditionally furnished. The Colón was a favourite of the artist Joan Miró and remains a Barcelona classic with a faithful following.

€€ Hotel Neri. ▬ *Sant Sever 5, Tel: 933 040 655, www.hotel neri.com, 22 rooms, Metro: Jaume 1, Liceu. Map p. 49, E2.*
A contemporary interior in an 18th-century townhouse, the Hotel Neri fuses tradition and modern design in a quiet square at the heart of the Gothic quarter, a stone's throw from the cathedral cloister and a short walk from the Rambla. The rooftop terrace is the place for breakfast or an evening *copa* up at bell tower level. The guest rooms (and one suite) are stylish, with light grey walls, dark wood furnishings and marble bathrooms. The luminous exterior rooms can be noisy in the morning when school begins across the square below. The more spacious rooms on the top three floors, with floor-to-ceiling windows overlooking the square, are the ones to ask for.

€€ Hotel Omm. ▬ *Carrer Rosselló 265, Tel: 934 454 000, www.hotel omm.es, 140 rooms, Metro: Diagonal. Map p. 96, C3.*
Designed by architect Juli Capella and interior designers Sandra Tarruella and Isabel López as a sleek three-dimensional zen mantra, the Omm even has Phillip Glass telephone waiting music. The restaurant, Moo, run by the famous Roca brothers of Girona's Michelin-starred Celler de Can Roca, serves exciting original creations. The hotel bar draws a dazzling crowd of Barcelona's postgraduate *crème de la crème.* Dark, slender hallways burst into clean-lined, well-lit rooms with views over interior courtyards and Passeig de Gràcia.

€ Hotel Banys Orientals. *Carrer Argenteria 37, Tel: 932 688 460, www.hotelbanys orientals.com, 43 rooms, Metro: Jaume 1. Map p. 74, A2.*
A minute's walk from the Santa Maria del Mar basilica (*see p. 76*), this is a perfect location for exploring many of early Barcelona's finest treasures, including the Picasso Museum (*see p. 79*), Carrer Montcada, and the Born area. A contemporary design exercise with graceful lighting and imaginative details such as Gaudí-esque chairs. The always packed

Stark interiors at the compact Chic and Basic Born hotel

Senyor Parellada restaurant downstairs offers good dining.

€ Chic & Basic Born. 🚇 *Carrer Princesa 50, Tel: 932 954 652, www.chicandbasic.com, 31 rooms, Metro: Arc de Triomf, Jaume I. Map p. 74, A3.* Freestanding glass shower stalls in the middle of the rooms let you know right away that this is a hotel with attitude (*pictured above*). A hit with art and design buffs looking for Barcelona's edgy cool at less than budget-bashing prices, the Chic & Basic hotels (there is another on Carrer Tallers) have brought designer Xavier Claramunt instant success in this design-voracious environment. The restaurant, The White Bar, serves creditable Mediterranean fare while the neighbourhood, with the Picasso Museum (*see p. 79*) a step away, is Barcelona at its purest. Corner rooms have better light and views; interior rooms over the patio are quieter.

€ Hostal Gat Xino. *Carrer Hospital 155, Tel: 933 248 833, www.gataccommodation.com, 35 rooms, Metro: Liceu, Sant Antoni. Map p. 22, D2.* For an oasis of clean-lined contemporary design in what was once (and to some degree still is) the rough and tumble Raval, this budget choice is at once a welcome relief from the street scene raging outside, and a chance to get to know Barcelona's most culturally diverse neighbourhood. Rooms are bright and colourful, the value is unbeatable for the central location, and, in the best hostal tradition, fellow guests often speak to one another.

€ Hotel Granados 83. ▪ *Carrer Enric Granados 83, Tel: 934 929 670, www.derbyhotels.com, 77 rooms, Metro: Diagonal, Provença. Map p. 96, C2.* Encased in glass, steel and exposed brick, this sleek contemporary building is at once redolent of an industrial complex and a Buddhist retreat. In what could be construed as an homage to Catalan composer Enric Granados with a touch of Asian exotica in the middle of the checkerboard Eixample, Hindu and Buddhist artworks from as early as the 10th century decorate both rooms and public spaces. The hotel restaurant opens onto a verdant terrace in an interior patio. The spacious, clean-lined rooms are equipped with the latest technology, including flat screen televisions and jacuzzis in the marble bathrooms. The four first-floor duplex suites share a semi-private pool and garden.

€ Hotel Villa Emilia. ▪ *Carrer Calabria 115–117, Tel: 932 525 285, www.hotelvillaemilia.com, 53 rooms, Metro: Rocafort. Off map p. 96.* Opened in 2006, this design hotel offers impeccable lodging at reasonable rates. Fully endowed with technological resources ranging from Wi-Fi connections to a business centre, the hotel is equidistant from Sants train station and Plaça Espanya, with the rest of the Eixample and the Rambla just a 20-minute walk or a five-minute Metro ride away. The lush 7th-floor roof terrace, though with no pool, is a popular spot for breakfast in the summer and drinks in the sun year round. The rooms on the 6th floor have less noise.

Apartments

Barcelona has a number of options for renting apartments. One good choice is Barcelona Rentals with apartments in historic city centre buildings which are family-owned and pleasantly furnished: www.atlanta-ads.com.

history

Ancient Barcelona

590 BC Greeks land in northern Catalonia and establish a colony, Emporión

3rd century BC The Laietani, an agricultural people, populate Montjuïc hill, calling the settlement Barkena

218 BC The Roman army lands in northern Catalonia at the start of the Second Punic War, in which Rome and Carthage dispute military and commercial control of the Mediterranean

133 BC Barcelona becomes part of the Roman Empire as Colonia Favencia Julia Augusta Paterna Barcino, part of Roman Hispania Citerior

AD 304 Santa Eulàlia martyred after being tortured and put to death by Roman governor Dacian, for refusing to renounce her Christian faith; she becomes one of Barcelona's patron saints

415 Visigoths, led by Ataulfo, take Barcelona. Ataulfo is murdered soon after

589 Visigoths consolidate control of Iberian Peninsula with their capital at Toledo

711 Moorish invasion of Iberian Peninsular

720 Moors consolidate control of all Iberian Peninsular through a series of pacts and tributary agreements

Medieval city

801 Barcelona freed from Moorish rule by Franks who make Catalonia part of the Marca Hispánica or Spanish March, a buffer zone against the Moorish Al-Andalus

985 Moors sack Barcelona, destroying Christian sites

988 Catalonia becomes an independent federal region after Charlemagne's Frankish heirs give no support against the Moors

1137 Ramon Berenguer IV, Sovereign Count-King of Barcelona, marries Petronila, the infant daughter of King Ramiro II of

Aragon, allying Catalonia with the landlocked Kingdom of Aragon. This alliance aids Catalonia's rise in the Mediterranean but would eventually lead to political eclipse after Aragon's union with the Spanish realms of Castile and León

Mediterranean Empire

1229 Jaume I conquers Majorca, the first of Catalonia's colonies

1265 Jaume I establishes Europe's first proto-democratic representative governing body, Barcelona's Consell de Cent (Council of One Hundred; *see p. 60*)

1283 The Corts de Barcelona, forerunner of the Generalitat, is convened to govern Catalonia

1329 Construction of Santa Maria del Mar basilica begins, dedicated to the protection of sailors; it is built in a record 54 years

1469 Ferdinand II of Aragon marries Isabella of Castile. Royal power begins to shift away from Catalonia

1492 Ferdinand and Isabella defeat the Moors at Granada, uniting all of Spain. Columbus discovers the New World, which becomes Spain's new focus, leaving Catalonia, excluded from trade there, to ply the Mediterranean. Drassanes Reials shipyards (*see p. 36*) continue to build much of Catalonia's merchant fleet

1561 Philip II makes Madrid his capital. Barcelona loses more influence

1640 First fortress built on Montjuïc hill (*see p. 130*) during the Guerra dels Segadors (War of the Reapers), a rebellion against Spanish King Felipe IV

War & Industrialisation

1714 War of the Spanish Succession won by the Bourbon contender Philip of Anjou (Felipe V), whom Barcelona did not support. Barcelona completely subjugated

1808 Napoleon occupies Barcelona during the Peninsular War; he turns the Monestir de Pedralbes (*see p. 111*) into his barracks

1844 Liceu opera house (*see p. 29*) construction begins

1860 Ildefons Cerdà wins the competition to design Barcelona's expansion out from the old city; the Neoclassical grid known as the Eixample district takes form

1873–74 Spain briefly proclaims herself a republic, while Catalonia claims autonomy

1878 The Sala Parés art gallery (*see p. 72*) opens, exhibiting every contemporary Barcelona artist of note: Pablo Picasso, Joan Miró, Ramon Casas, Santiago Rusiñol, Isidre Nonell

1882 Work begins on the Sagrada Família (*see p. 99*) under Francesc Villar; a year later Antoni Gaudí takes over

1890 'Gold fever' (*'febre d'or'*) hits the Eixample and construction skyrockets; most of the district's *Modernista* architecture is built over the next two decades

1914 The Mancomunitat, Catalonia's representative body, is set up

1926 Antoni Gaudí is hit by a tram and later dies in the Hospital de la Santa Creu i Sant Pau (*see p. 36*)

1931 Second Spanish Republic proclaimed after national referendum votes out the monarchy and Alfonso XIII abdicates. The Generalitat again governs Catalonia

1936–39 Spanish Civil War breaks out when the forces of the Spanish right rebel against the increasingly leftist, though legitimately elected, government

1939–75 The Franco regime's National Movement represses Catalonia politically, culturally and linguistically as never before

1975 Franco dies. King Juan Carlos I succeeds Franco regency as head of state

A modern state

1978 Spanish Constitution approved. Extensive home rule granted to 13 autonomous communities in a constitutional monarchy under King Juan Carlos I

1992 Barcelona hosts the Olympic Games. Catalan confidence high

2000 King Juan Carlos celebrates 25 years as Spain's king

2006 Catalonia's controversial new Autonomy Statute, granting greater control over local revenues and infrastructure as well as more protection for the Catalan language, is approved by the socialist government of José Luis Rodríguez Zapatero

2008 President José Luis Rodríguez Zapatero again wins elections and forms Europe's first government with a majority of women holding ministerial posts

LA RAMBLA
& EL RAVAL

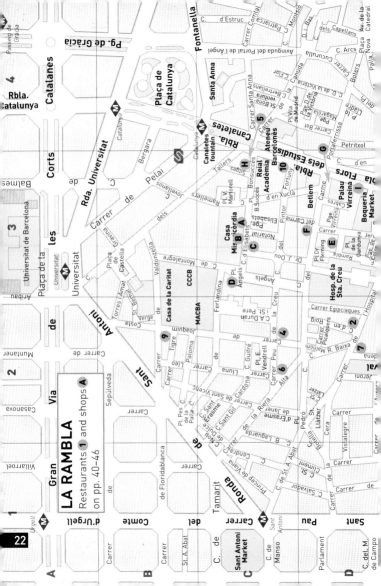

LA RAMBLA

Restaurants **1** and shops **A**
on pp. 40–46

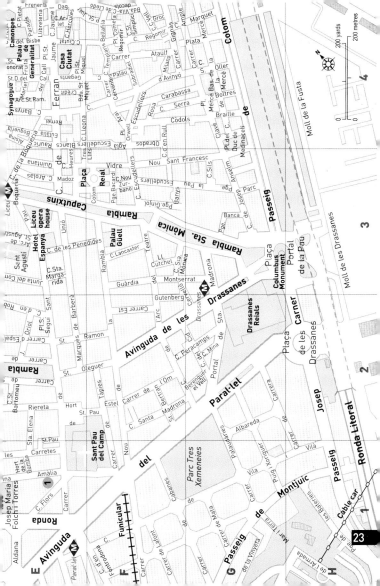

introduction

Barcelona's Rambla, described by Spanish poet Federico García Lorca as 'the only street I ever wished would never end' is famed far and wide as the city's most characteristic promenade. In contrast, El Raval, the area to the west of the Rambla on the right as you walk toward the port, was originally a slum or *arrabal* outside the 13th-century walls. It used to be notorious for its Barrio Chino red-light district, the lurid attractions of which are known to have fascinated, among others, the young Pablo Picasso. Today, the Raval has been largely, though by no means completely, gentrified by the gleaming Museu d'Art Contemporani de Barcelona (MACBA), and the equally dazzling Centre de Cultura Contemporània de Barcelona (CCCB). The Hospital de la Santa Creu, the pre-Romanesque Sant Pau del Camp church, Gaudí's Palau Güell, and the Hotel Espanya are the main attractions in the Raval, while back on the Rambla, the Liceu opera house, Boqueria market and the Reials Drassanes medieval shipyards are all quintessential Barcelona sites.

The Rambla

Map: p. 22, C4 **Highlights:** Boqueria market; Liceu opera house

A plane tree-covered catwalk over a kilometre long, the Rambla is an all-purpose pedestrian promenade, pavement café, press kiosk, flower stall and 24-hour street theatre. Some 50 metres wide, the Rambla descends from Plaça Catalunya to the harbour. Originally a dry water-course that drained the Collserola hills that rise behind the city, this sandy crease ran just outside the 13th-century city walls. Over the centuries it became a beehive of extramural activity, attracting humanity in all its glorious diversity: journeyman workers, costermongers, butchers, vendors, quacks, scam artists, pickpockets and preachers. By the time the walls were torn down in the late 17th century, the Rambla had become essential to the life of the city and was left open as a thorough-fare, meeting place and promenade.

The Rambla today is the place to stroll en route to the Raval or the Gothic quarter, but also has its own share of attractions:

❶ Canaletes fountain: Once dispensing the purest water in the city, chanelled from high in the Pyrenees, the fountain is now a focal point for FC Barcelona fans celebrating their football team's latest victory, and for the romantic myth that those who drink from the fountain are destined to fall in love with the city and always return.

❷ Reial Acadèmia de Ciències i Arts de Barcelona: Home to the Teatre Poliorama since 1906, the clock on the ornate façade has been Barcelona's official time-keeper since 1891. In *Homage to Catalonia*, George Orwell tells of his time observing street fighting from the roof in 1937 during the Civil War.

❸ Betlem church: The only remaning Jesuit institution in the city after the order's expulsion from Spain in 1767. On medieval foundations, the impressive—and well-preserved—18th-century Baroque façade (on Carrer del Carme) shows the founder of the Jesuit Order, St Ignatius Loyola (on the left of the door), and a later leader of the Jesuits, San Francisco de Borja (on the right) carrying a skull and Bible, symbols of his rejection of worldly things.

The Rambla

Café Viena
(*see p. 44*)

1 Canaletes fountain
2 Reial Acadèmia de Ciénces
   i Arts de Barcelona
3 Betlem Church
4 Palau Virreina

Antiga Casa
Figueres
(*see p. 43*)

Centre d'Art de
Santa Monica

Plaça Reial
(*see p. 62*)

5 Boqueria market
6 Miró mosaic
7 Liceu opera house
8 Columbus statue

Drassanes
shipyards
(*see p. 36*)

The Ramblas dissected

Often cited in the plural as 'Las Ramblas', this teeming thoroughfare is unofficially divided into five sections defined by the medieval gates of the city walls:

Ⓐ Rambla de les Canaletes: Named for the canals that once brought water from the source of the Llobregat river in the Pyrenees to the Canaletes fountain (*see previous page*)

Ⓑ Rambla dels Estudis: Referring to the university classrooms located here until they were punitively banished by Felipe V because of anti-Castilian activity in the early 18th century. This part of the Rambla is now more commonly called Rambla dels Ocells (birds) for its bird market

Ⓒ Rambla de les Flors: Perhaps the most romantic section of the Rambla, named for the flower sellers who have traded here since the 13th century, and where the *Modernista* artist Ramon Casas first glimpsed his favourite muse (and future wife) selling flowers in the late 1800s. This section is also known as Rambla de Sant Josep for the Carmelite convent which was 'excloistered' in 1836 and subsequently demolished, making space for the first stalls of the Boqueria market (*see p. 28*)

Ⓓ Rambla dels Caputxins: The name of this section of the Rambla is taken from the Capuchin monastery that stood here until the late 18th century

Ⓔ Rambla de Santa Mònica: Opposite the medieval shipyards Drassanes Reials (*see p. 36*), this was the first section of the Rambla to become popular as an aristocratic promenade, in the 18th century. It was named after the Santa Mònica convent (1618), the oldest structure still remaining on the Rambla, and now a bookshop and modern art gallery

❹ Palau Virreina: The grandest palace on the Rambla, it was completed in 1778 for Spain's Viceroy in Peru, Manuel Amat i Junyent, and is now popularly named after the Viceroy's widow, La Virreina, who became an important city benefactress. Now the palace houses the Institut de Cultura, with a good bookshop.

❺ Boqueria market: (*open Mon–Sat 8–4, Tel: 933 182 017, an information kiosk is in aisle no. 7 at stand no. 435, near the Bar Boqueria; for eating, see p. 43; Metro: Liceu*). Europe's oldest operating city centre produce market, accompanies Gaudí's Sagrada Familia (*see p. 99*) and Santa Maria del Mar (*see p. 76*) among the city's top three delights. Surrounded by the Doric columns that ringed what the architect, Francesc Daniel Molina, conceived as a Neoclassical square (not unlike his Plaça Reial; *see p. 62*), the market sprouted and grew in this open space from the late 19th century. Today, the space is packed with early-rising top local chefs and residents, and later with a throng of visitors keen to experience the assault on all the senses that La Boqueria provides. The vegetable, fruit and wild mushroom display at the entrance is the most colourful painting in town while the chilly circular fish and seafood amphitheatre in the heart of the market provides a complete course in Mediterranean and Atlantic ichthyology. The Jesús y Carmen stand (no. 580) is a living, three-dimensional Van Gogh still-life starring ropes of peppers from all over the world, along with nuts, vegetables, exquisite new potatoes and every manner of dry goods impeccably arranged. Near the popular Kiosko Universal (*see p. 43*) restaurant counter, the Avinova Serramitjana stand (no. 689) is the place, in hunting season, to have a look at the redleg partridge, woodcock, duck and hare. Petràs, at the back of the market (no. 870), is an educational observation of wild mushrooms, spices and herbs from Catalonia and countries all around the world. Morels, chanterelles, *rovellons*, *camagrocs*, truffles, *ous de reig* (king's testicles), *trompetes de la mort* (trumpets of death) *pets de llop* (wolf farts)—you name it, Llorenç Petràs will have it if it has surfaced anywhere on the planet.

❻ Miró mosaic: In the centre of the Rambla is an expansive mosaic by the Catalan artist Joan Miró, who was born and had a studio nearby, at Passatge del Crédit 4 (*map p. 49, F2*). The mosaic was unveiled in 1976 as part of a project by the painter to display as much of his art as possible in the streets of Barcelona.

7 Liceu opera house: (*guided tours daily at 10, entry charge, Tel: 934 859 900, www.liceu barcelona.com, Metro: Liceu*). Overlooking the heart of the thronging Rambla, Barcelona's opera house may seem plain from the outside, but the glittering salons within confirm its fame as one of Europe's most beautiful opera venues. With superb acoustics and a seating capacity second only to Milan's La Scala, Barcelona's most cherished bourgeois playroom, once a Trinitarian monastery, has had an unfortunate history of natural and unnatural disasters. After its original construction in 1844 it was badly damaged by fire and had to be completely rebuilt by Josep Oriol Mestres (who also designed the neo-Gothic façade of the cathedral; *see p. 51*), and then disaster struck again when it was gutted in a blaze in 1861. When the Liceu was finally completed, it quickly became the focal point of social contact for

Barcelona's opera-obsessed elite. Barcelona lacked a royal court: there were no king's *levées* for ambitious young men to attend, no palace balls for debutantes to make their society entrances. Instead they came to the Liceu: to see and be seen, to further their careers, to flirt and find marriage partners, to hatch plots and intrigues. It was here that Isabel López, daughter of shipping magnate Marqués de Comillas Antonio López y López, met her future husband, and Gaudí's patron, Eusebi Güell. The Liceu's bad fortune was to continue, when in 1893 the opera house was bombed by anarchists, and in 1994 the building was once again gutted by a blaze. Five years later, restored as far as possible to its former glory, supremely equipped for modern productions, the Liceu opened anew. Even if you don't see an opera here, don't miss a tour of the building; some of the Liceu's most spectacular rooms (including the glittering foyer known as the Saló dels Miralls, or Hall of Mirrors) were untouched by the 1994 fire, as were those of Spain's oldest social club, El Cercle del Liceu. The Cercle's dozen Ramon Casas paintings are all brilliantly illuminated in the club's penumbral smoking room and comprise Barcelona's best Casas stash. If you love opera, the Espai Liceu shop downstairs is the place to browse. There is also a 50-seat concert hall, and a mediatheque featuring recordings and films of past productions.

❽ Columbus monument: (*open daily 10–8.30, entry charge, Metro: Drassanes*). Sixty metres up, Columbus stands tall at the foot of the Rambla pointing out to the Mediterranean; the key to Barcelona's trading prosperity and power (Catalonia was banned from New World trade by the Spanish crown after Columbus returned from America). The Drassanes shipyard built two of the boats in Columbus's fleet. The column was erected in 1888 with, at that time, a unique lift-shaft installed inside. A trip up to the viewing platform offers unique views of the city and out to sea.

Palau Güell

*Palau Güell is only partly open until 2010 while restoration work is carried out. Temporary opening hours are: Mon–Sat 10–2.30, closed Sun. While restoration continues entry is free.***Tel:** 933 173 974
Metro: Drassanes, Liceu **Map:** p. 23, F3
Highlights: Gothic-inspired façade; reception room ceilings

Palau Güell may be considered the mature Gaudí's official launching and was a bold beginning for the young architect's first commission from the man destined to become his main patron, Eusebi Güell. The palace was officially opened in 1888, to coincide with the city's World Exhibition, and initial reactions were mixed. Some thought it 'Babylonian' others 'dungeon-like' (somewhat prophetic in that the basement was used as a Republican secret-police prison during the Civil War). Gaudí patiently insisted that 'Count Güell and I like it', but it is known that the Countess, Isabel López, hated it and was frightened to walk around the rooms at night.

The looming Gothic **façade** evokes a medieval baronial hall with its imposing parabolic arches forming the entrance-way and elaborate

The twin entranceways at Palau Güell with the patron's initials on each

ironwork incorporating Eusebi Güell's initials (*pictured above*). The ceramic polychrome chimneys on the roof (just visible from the pavement) are the only colour on the exterior.

Inside, columns shaped like wild mushrooms form a system of parabolic arches that support the entire building. The interior patio, where the horses were groomed, receives light through a skylight, one of numerous devices Gaudí used to illuminate this tenebrous edifice. Other tricks include mirrors and frosted-glass panels placed over artificial light sources. The chutes on the Carrer Nou de la Rambla side of the basement were for delivering horse fodder straight in from street level overhead, while the steep spiral ramp was the servants' access to the main entrance hall. The pine-block paving on the ground-floor entranceway was used instead of cobblestones to muffle the sound of horses' hooves.

Upstairs, the three **reception rooms** contain wooden ceilings progressing from merely splendid to Byzantine in the complexity of their moulded floral and leaf motifs. The third reception room, with the most elaborate ceiling ornamentation, has a latticed *jalousie* in the gallery above, a double screen behind which Count Güell was able to inspect and, almost literally, eavesdrop on his visitors. The central salon has a three-storey parabolic cupola, lined with alabaster, which reaches up above the roofline. This was the grand hall, used for parties, receptions and musical evenings (not dances—polite Barcelona society in those days frowned on dancing for young ladies). Musicians played from the balcony, and the overhead balcony window was for the main vocalist. A chapel of beaten copper with retractable kneeling pads and a small two-seater bench built into the right side of the altar is enclosed behind a double door. Around the corner is a small organ, the pipes in rectangular tubes climbing the central gallery.

The dining room has a *Modernista* fireplace in the shape of a deeply curving horseshoe arch at one end. The long bench and sitting area under the window boasts upholstery and carpeting that looks forward to the fashions of the 1970s. The louvred window blinds and mechanism for adjusting their angle are the originals. From the outside rear terrace, the polished grey marble of the main part of the house is visible. The marble came from Count Güell's own quarry in El Garraf, just south of Barcelona. The servants' quarters, made of brick, rise up on the left. A passageway built out toward the Rambla linked Palau Güell with the Count's father's house, which overlooked the Rambla dels Caputxins.

Upstairs again are the bedrooms of Count Güell and his wife, Isabel López, and the couple's bathroom, appointed with all the modern conveniences of the late 19th century.

On the roof, the colourful and playful Gaudí of Park Güell (*see p. 112*) and Casa Batlló (*see p. 104*) is fully exposed in his 20 polychrome *trencadís* chimneys. The main chimney supports a weathervane in the form of a bat, the emblem of Jaume I el Conqueridor, the sovereign count who conquered Majorca and paved the way for Catalonia's Mediterranean empire. Count-King Jaume is said to have chosen the bat as his emblem after his Majorca campaign, when a bat fluttering in his tent woke him in time to alert his troops to a pre-dawn Moorish assault. Jaume I's Catalan bat can also be sighted on the façade of the Hospital de la Santa Creu i Sant Pau over Carrer Hospital (*see p. 36*).

Museu d'Art Contemporani de Barcelona (MACBA) ← *check exhibit*

Open: Mon & Wed–Fri 11–7.30, Sat 10–8, Sun 10–3 **Charges:** Entry charge with reduced fee on Wed; free guided tours available daily **Tel:** 934 120 810 **Web:** www.macba.es **Metro:** Catalunya, Sant Antoni, Universitat **Map:** p. 22, C2
Highlights: Richard Meier architecture; Catalan collection

The bright, open space at the end of Carrer Elisabets is filled with the white-tiled, glass and plastic contemporary art gallery designed by the American architect Richard Meier in 1992. This gleaming explosion of light and geometry in the once-penumbral Raval houses a permanent collection of contemporary art as well as travelling exhibits. With a sly wink to Gaudí (the irregular tower in front of the main façade), Meier's immaculate Rationalist structure has always been a subject of controversy among numerous Barcelona design professionals and aficionados. Basque sculptor Jorge Oteiza's massive bronze *La Ola* (The Wave) on MACBA's front porch is a popular gathering point for skateboard surfers, while Eduardo Chillida's *Barcelona* climbs the wall to the left of the main entrance. MACBA's collection of 20th-century art is excellent, focusing on Catalan and Spanish artists, as well as including international works such as the sculptures of Alexander Calder and Robert Rauschenberg. The free guided tour is equally insightful.

Directly across from the main entrance to MACBA is the chapel of the **Convent dels Àngels** (*opening times as MACBA, Tel: 934 437 520, www.fadweb.org*). This former Augustinian convent, built by Bartomeu Roig in the middle of the 16th century, is currently the headquarters for Foment dels Arts Decoratives (FAD) which runs this cultural centre. The exhibition hall, called the Fòrum dels Àngels, has beautifully carved and restored sculptures of angels in the interior, while the centre also boasts a bookstore, a 150-seat auditorium, and a restaurant and bar.

in the area

Casa de la Misericòrdia (*Metro: Catalunya*). Buildings surround an ivy-covered courtyard with shady palm trees at what was once a home and school for orphans and girls from poor families, transforming many who 'might otherwise have perished in poverty or stumbled into the pitfalls of immorality' into 'useful and productive women', as one historian put it. The complex also included a foundling hospice. Around the corner to the right of the main entrance is a wooden porthole set into the wall. This is an ancient *torno* or turntable, where, up until well into the 20th century, unwanted babies were spun into the safe arms of the nuns of the House of Mercy. Now cemented in, this wooden oval once contained a partitioned revolving shelf. In response to the knock of a woman in distress, the nun on duty would answer 'Ave Maria', to which the new mother replied in kind as the turntable creaked her newborn out of one troubled life and into another. The coin slot above to the left was used for contributions to the hospice. The site is now a municipal office but it is possible to look into the courtyard. **Map p. 22, C3**

Centre de Cultura Contemporània de Barcelona (CCCB) (*Tues–Fri 11-2 & 4-8, Wed & Sat 11-8, Sun 11-7, entry charge but free entry to patio and bookstore, Tel: 933 064 100, www.cccb.org, Metro: Catalunya, Sant Antoni, Universitat*). In the Casa de la Caritat, behind MACBA (*see p. 33*), is the restored and remodelled Centre de Cultura Contemporània de Barcelona (CCCB) in a former medieval convent and hospital. The main courtyard, Pati de les Dones or Women's Courtyard, is one of Barcelona's best marriages of traditional architecture and contemporary design. Architects Albert Vilaplana and Helio Piñón have installed an upper right-hand patio wall made of smoked glass and angled to reflect views of Montjuïc park and the Mediterranean into what was once a gated nunnery (*pictured opposite*). The CCCB hosts concerts, lectures, art shows and exhibitions of all kinds. **Map p. 22, B3**

The beautiful mixture of traditional and modern architecture in the former medieval convent which now houses Barcelona's centre of culture (CCCB)

a/s/e Barcelona

Drassanes Reials (*open daily 10–8, closed 25 & 26 Dec, 1 & 6 Jan, entry charge except after 3pm on first Sat of month, Tel: 933 429 920, www.museumaritimbarcelona.org, Metro: Drassanes at the Portal de Santa Madrona exit*). At the port end of the Rambla on Plaça del Portal de la Pau, the medieval shipyards house Barcelona's excellent Maritime Museum in a superb example of late 14th-century Catalan Gothic architecture. The best-preserved medieval shipyards in the world, topping even Venice's Arsenale, the Drassanes built the ships of Catalonia's Mediterranean fleet and launched them directly down their slipways into the sea (today's quay which leaves the Drassanes high and dry is post-18th-century landfill). The shipyards marked the waterside edge of 14th-century Barcelona. Outside Drassanes, on the Avinguda del Paral.lel side, is an intact section of the city's third and final set of 14th- to 15th-century city walls. **Map p. 23, G2**

Hospital de la Santa Creu i Sant Pau (*Biblioteca de Catalunya open Mon–Fri 9–8, Sat 9–2, guided tours available at the main desk; Convalescence House open daily 9–2, Tel: 932 701 620 for guided tour; Royal Academy of Surgery and Medicine open Thur only; entrances at Casa de la Convalescència on Carrer del Carme or through the main door on Carrer Hospital, Metro: Liceu*). Descended from a 10th-century hospice, most of the present buildings and courtyards of the Hospital de la Santa Creu i Sant Pau (Hospital of the Holy Cross and of Saint Paul) were built in the 15th and 16th centuries. From Carrer Hospital, you can see the oldest section of the medieval hospital, part of the old Hospital de Colom founded in 1219, with small grated windows and nearly completely disintegrated decorative sculptures from the original building. The heraldry over the main door includes, at the top, the ubiquitous bat, favourite emblem of Jaume I (also at Palau Güell; *see p. 30*). The Reial Acadèmia de Cirurgia i Medecina (**Royal Academy of Surgery and Medicine**) is a Neoclassical 18th-century building of carved stone which contains an amphitheatre originally used for the observation of dissections. The patio of the 17th-century Casa de la Convalescència (**Convalescence House**) has Renaissance columns and brightly decorated scenes of the life of St Paul in the vestibule. The image of St Paul in the centre of the courtyard honours the building's initial benefactor, Pau (Paul) Ferran. Look for the horseshoes (*ferradura*) around the keyholes on the double wooden doors in the entryway, a semantic reminder of benefactor Ferran. The 1.5-million-volume **Biblioteca de Catalunya** is the national library of Catalonia and Spain's second largest after Madrid's Biblioteca Nacional. Inside the library, the wide Gothic arches and vaulting of what was once the hospital's main nave were designed in the 15th century by Guillem Abiell, the architect of Santa Maria del Pi church (*see p. 62*), who was seeking light and a sense of space here. This was the hospital where Antoni Gaudí was taken after he was struck by a tram on 7th June 1926. Among the library's collections are archives recording Gaudí's admittance, and photographs of the infirmary and the private room where he died. The library's staggering resources range from silver medieval book covers to illuminated manuscripts from the *Llibre Vermell* (Red Book), a 14th-century collection of Catalonian pilgrim songs. **Map p. 22, D3**

Hotel Espanya (*Tel: 933 181 758, www.hotelespanya.com, Metro: Liceu*). Just off the Rambla is the spectacular *Modernista* hotel La Fonda Espanya built by Lluís Domènech i Montaner, architect of the Palau de la Música Catalana (*see p. 57*). Oddly, for a city obsessed with its *Modernista* treasures, the present-day hotel is surprisingly down at heel, though a restoration and refurbishing programme is planned. Recipient of the 1903 prize for the best architectural creation of the year, this classic gem merits careful exploration. The breakfast room is dominated by an enormous marble mantelpiece sculpted by *Modernista* master Eusebi Arnau. An allegory for

The Ramon Casas mermaid murals are a star feature at Hotel Espanya

the passage of time and of life itself, a mother holds her baby on one side while an aged man stretches his hands toward the flame from the other, while cats warm themselves on the hearth. The chimney breast displays Spain's royal escutcheon: the double-headed eagle of the Holy Roman Empire, and the Order of the Golden Fleece hanging below it, a chivalric order founded by Philip the Good of Burgundy in 1429, and which survived in Spain until Alfonso XIII's abdication in 1931. The restaurant, nearly always empty, is richly endowed with colourful renderings of the coats of arms of Spain's different provinces and regions. Beyond that is the famous Ramon Casas aquarium dining room (*pictured on previous page*), with murals of long-legged, flipper-shod mermaids and Mediterranean aquatic life. This stands over a wooden lattice-work dado with ceramic tiles bearing provincial coats of arms from the four corners of Spain. **Map p. 23, E3**

Sant Antoni market (*open Mon–Thurs & Sat 7–2.30 & 5.30–8.30, Fri 7am–8.30pm, Tel: 934 437 520, Metro: Sant Antoni*). An interesting spot to browse through, as much for its artistic value as for the potpourri of produce on sale, the Mercat Sant Antoni, reminiscent of La Boqueria before it became Europe's most celebrated food fair, is one of Barcelona's hidden gems. This mammoth steel hangar was designed in 1882 by Antoni Rovira i Trias, the real winner of the competition for the planning of Barcelona's Eixample (eventually awarded to the Madrid-imposed urban planner Ildefons Cerdà; *see p. 138*). Considered the city's greatest masterpiece of ironwork architecture, the Greek-cross-shaped market covers an entire block. A combination of food, clothing and flea market, it becomes a book, comics, stamp, and coin fest on Sundays. Though many of the food produce stalls inside remain closed, a stroll through the market will reveal excellent bars and restaurants and some of the finest *Modernista* stall façades in Barcelona. **Map p. 22, C1**

Sant Pau del Camp (*cloister open Tues–Sat 10.30–1 & Mon–Fri 5–8pm, Sunday mass 12 & 8pm, Metro: Paral.lel*). Sant Pau del Camp (St Paul's in the Fields), Barcelona's oldest church (*pictured right*), was built outside the second set of city walls on the site of a 2nd-century Roman cemetery later used by Christian Visigoths. After the Moors sacked Barcelona in 985 and 1115, destroying Christian sites, Sant Pau del Camp was built in 1127, its hunched, cowering shape reflecting the defensive spirit of the besieged early medieval Christians. The main entrance is composed of 6th- or 7th-century Visigothic marble capitals atop recycled Roman columns. The tympanum shows Christ in Majesty between Saints Peter

Sant Pau del Camp, Barcelona's oldest church, looks remote but is actually on the edge of the busy Raval district

and Paul. The symbols and images above seem to date from an earlier epoch in which human images were avoided, possibly the work of Mudéjar artisans. The Divine hand, two fingers extended, centres the façade with the symbols of the Evangelists Matthew (angel/human) and John (eagle). Inside the church is a sepulchral slab from the tomb of Sovereign Count Guifré II, dated 912, evidence that a 10th-century chapel existed on this site. The stained glass window overlooking the Carrer de Sant Pau side of the apse is Barcelona's smallest, bookend to Santa Maria del Pi's largest (*see p. 62*), while the bevelled window apertures seem as much arrow slits as windows, reinforcing the fortress aspect of pre-Romanesque liturgical architecture. The diminutive cloister is Sant Pau del Camp's best secret, a miniature gem and one of Barcelona's finest hideaways. The tri-lobed arches, clearly of Moorish descent, are supported by carved Corinthian capitals portraying Adam and Eve, an archer shooting at a gazelle, and a woman tormented by toads, among other themes. Surrounded by the raucous Raval and the din of Avinguda del Paral.lel beyond, this intimate cloister is an acoustic oasis and a pocket of peace.
Map p. 23, F1

eat

The Rambla has a reputation for dismal food dished out at the pavement cafés. However, Café Viena's *ibérico* ham sandwich is outstanding as a lunchtime snack, and the Boqueria market offers several reputable counters and bars, starring Pinotxo and Quim de la Boqueria. The Raval is the place to look for restaurants, from the excellent Ca l'Isidre to Casa Leopoldo or La Reina del Raval on the new Rambla del Raval. For price categories, see p. 11; all restaurants are located on map pp. 22 & 23.

1 €€€ Ca l'Isidre, *Les Flors 12, Tel: 934 411 139, open 1–4 & 8–midnight, closed Sun, Christmas, Easter & 3 weeks in Aug, Metro: Paral.lel.* ■
Long a favourite with the power elite from King Juan Carlos to Barcelona artists from the late Joan Miró to young superstar Joan Pere Viladecans. The walls of this classic, somewhat formal, Catalan cuisine sanctuary are covered with pictures and engravings by Dalí amongst others. Two steps from the Sant Pau del Camp church (*see p. 38*), the traditional Catalan country cooking prepared here is based on the fresh produce carefully selected by Isidre soon after sunrise at the nearby Boqueria market (*see p. 28*). Much of the fare reflects the owner's passions and pastimes: stewed redleg partridge (often bagged by Isidre himself) from October to February, *estofada de toro de lidia* (stewed fighting bull) carefully marinated and cooked slowly, in summer a chilled *gazpacho* with a fresh shrimp or two and a dollop of virgin olive oil, chick peas with baby squid, duck liver, duck breast, foie gras ravioli, or roast sea bass. If *espardenyes* (known as sea cucumbers, but more like a cuttlefish than a vegetable) are on the menu, don't hesitate to try this Mediterranean delicacy typical of the Costa Brava.

2 €€ El Cafetí, *Carrer Hospital 99 (end of Passatge Bernardí Martorell), Tel: 933 292 419, open 1.30–4.30 & 8.30–1am, closed Mon, public hols & 3 weeks in Aug, Metro: Liceu.*
Candlelit and romantic, this little hideaway is an intimate bistro decorated in *Noucentiste* style. The menu covers an ample range of ingredients from rice dishes (13 different kinds) to the full anthology of Mediterranean fish. Try one of the many variations on the classic Spanish paella, or the *solomillo de corzo al foie* (roebuck filet with duck

liver) or *ensalada tibia de queso de cabra* (warm goat cheese salad).

③ €€ Casa Leopoldo, *Carrer San Rafael 24, Tel: 934 413 014, open 1–4 & 8–midnight, closed 1 week in Jan, Easter & Aug, Metro: Liceu.* ■ Just 100m east of the Rambla del Raval, Casa Leopoldo is famous for fine seafood and traditional Catalan fare. Once hidden in the labyrinthine streets west of the Rambla, this restaurant owned by the Gil family now overlooks a sunny construction site that will become a sleek new hotel. Owner Rosa Gil speaks six languages (English, German, Portuguese, Spanish, Catalan and French) and is a popular social and political mover and shaker in the Raval. The *revuelto de ajos tiernos y gambas* (eggs scrambled with young garlic and shrimp) or any of the fish specialities from *llobarro al forn* (baked sea bass) to *daurada a la sal* (gilthead bream cooked in salt) are recommended. Albarinos, Ruedas, Priorats and Montsants are among Rosa's top tips on her interesting wine list.

④ €€ La Casa de la Rioja, *Peu de la Creu 8–10, Tel: 934 433 363, open 1.30–4.30 & 8.30–midnight, Metro: Sant Antoni.* A combination restaurant and La Rioja cultural and tourism centre, this is a popular place with students, professors, museum staff, designers and people from all walks of Raval life looking for authentic and affordable cooking from Spain's most famous winegrowing region. La Rioja staples such as *patatas a la riojana* (potatoes stewed with chorizo sausage) or *caparrones de Anguiano estofados* (stewed pygmy beans from around the mountain village of Anguiano) are joined by more streamlined creations from La Nueva Cocina Riojana, modern La Rioja cooking as developed by new stars such as Francis Paniego and Marqués de Riscal.

⑤ €€ Julivert Meu, *Carrer Bonsuccés 7, Tel: 933 180 343, open Mon–Sat 1–1, Sun 1–4 & 8–1, closed Sun in Aug, Christmas, Metro: Catalunya.* Tight but cozy and rustic quarters in this old favourite just off the Rambla provide a fitting environ ment for the traditional Catalan cooking dished up at Julivert Meu ('my parsley' in Catalan). Along with Castilian specialities such as *jamón ibérico de bellota* (ham from a free range, acorn-fed, wild Iberian black pig) Catalan classics here include *esqueixada* (raw codfish with green and red peppers and aubergines), *escalivada* (vegetables roasted over coals) and meat cooked *a la brasa* (over coals). *Xatonada* (a salad with endives, cod, tuna, anchovies and a *xató* sauce of olive oil, garlic and almonds) is a Julivert Meu favourite.

⑥ €€ Mam i Teca, *Carrer Lluna 4, Tel: 934 413 335, open Mon, Wed–Fri & Sun 1–midnight, Sat 8.30–midnight, Metro: Sant Antoni.* ■ This intimate Raval tapas specialist takes its name from an archaic Catalan expression meaning 'food

Pinotxo bar, one of the best and friendliest counters at the Boqueria market

and drink', which fairly precisely communicates the general idea of this no-frills, no-nonsense yellow and green hideaway. *Botifarra* sausages, anchovies, shrimp with anything from asparagus to artichokes to broad beans in season, everything on the menu here is carefully thought out and prepared.

7 **€€ La Reina del Raval**, *Rambla del Raval 3, Tel: 934 433 655, open Tues-Fri 1.30-3.30 (Sat & Sun until 4.30), Tues-Sat 8.30-midnight, closed Mon, Sun evening, Metro: Liceu, Paral.lel.* The multicultural Raval at its most diverse and colourful passes by this upper corner of the relatively new Rambla del Raval. La Reina de Raval offers a reasonable lunch menu as well as a tasting menu that stand as two of the best quality and value dining opportunities in the Raval. *Foie micuit de Lara con trompetas* (homemade duck liver with wild mushrooms) as well as rice dishes ranging from *arròs a banda* (a fish broth paella) or *fideuà negre* (noodle paella cooked in squid ink) join fresh products from the nearby Boqueria market *(see p. 28)*. *Lubina al horno* (roast sea bass) and *pollo con setas* (chicken with wild mushrooms) are staples as well. Six bay windows overlook the Rambla del Raval while outside tables take prime sunlight from late morning until late afternoon. Cocktails, especially daiquiris, are much treasured in this sleek, modern design space.

●**€€ Boqueria market**, *Rambla 89* (**map p. 22, D3**), *Tel: 933 182 017, open Mon–Sat 8–4, Metro: Liceu*. The appetite-enhancing Boqueria market has eight tiny stands serving everything from simple beer and sandwiches to full scale gourmet cuisine. The three standouts are Pinotxo (*pictured opposite*), Quim de la Boqueria, and El Kiosko Universal. Of these three counters, Pinotxo and Quim de la Boqueria offer superior cooking and tastes, while El Kiosko Universal has more space in a sunny corner of the square under elegant Doric columns. Charismatic Juanito Bayén has been the never-changing face of **Pinotxo** ■ (and the Boqueria market for that matter) for so long that a lot of people think he is Pinotxo and call him such. Just inside the main Rambla entrance to the market, the dozen bar stools and four tables fill up quickly around the standard two o'clock Barcelona lunch hour. Juanito takes good care of new visitors as well as his perennial faithful. Place yourself in his hands and you can score a three-course lunch here, with the freshest jumbo shrimp or stewed *rape* (monkfish) you've ever tasted cooked fast, hot, salty and garlicky. Juanito's *mongetes de Santa Pau amb calamarsets* are legendary: small but intense white beans from the volcanic Garrotxa region of northern Catalonia stewed with baby cuttlefish. **Quim de la Boqueria** ■, closer to the centre of the fray, is known for its *ous esclafats amb llanqueta* (smashed fried eggs with a small Mediterranean fish), but everything served here is carefully prepared and exquisitely tasty. **El Kiosko Universal** serves creditable tapas and a fixed-price lunch menu with traditional standards such as grilled vegetables, wild mushrooms and fish specialities from sea bass to monkfish. With three dozen bar stools and another dozen tiny tables under the Neoclassical columns, El Kiosko Universal usually has live music and a young and jubilant crowd drawn by the good value, the rollicking vibe and the company of each other.

8 € Antiga Casa Figueres (currently Pasteleria Escribà), *Rambla 83, Tel: 933 016 027, open daily 9–9, Metro: Liceu*. Founded in 1820 and completely refurbished in 1902, the frontage of this cake and pastry emporium is pure *Modernista* Barcelona with its glinting, coloured mosaic tiles (*pictured overleaf*), stained-glass windows, and delicate ironwork; it's enough to catch your eye from the middle of the Rambla. Inside are pastries and chocolates to satisfy any sweet tooth and down the few steps are two or three tables where you can linger over coffee.

● **9 € Ca l'Estevet**, *Valdonzella 46, Tel: 933 024 186, open Mon–Sat 1–4 & 9–midnight, closed Sun, Metro: Universitat*. This romantic slot near the MACBA (*see p. 33*) has long been a favourite of students, journalists and artists. Across the street from Barcelona's journalism school, and around the block from the former home of Barcelona's *La Vanguardia* daily newspaper, Estevet has offered rock-bottom prices and much better than average Catalan cuisine for two generations. Estevet and family are invariably charming and gracious, and the carefully elaborated country cooking is, especially at these prices, always welcome. Try the asparagus cooked over coals, the *chopitos* (deep-fried baby cuttlefish), or the *magret de pato* (duck breast).

10 € Café Viena, *Rambla 115, Tel: 933 171 492, open daily 8am–11.30pm, Sat & Sun until 12.30am, Metro: Catalunya*. The 2006 announcement printed in the *New York Times* contending that Café Viena sells the world's best sandwich is plastered all over the façade and interior of this traditional Rambla favourite. For once, the *Times* might be right: the famous *flauta de pa amb tomàquet d'elaboració propia i pernil ibèric d.o. Jabugo (Huelva)* (flute of homemade bread spread with tomato squeezings and olive oil and *ibérico* ham from the Jabugo denomination of origin) appears to be the real thing. Whether the ham is the top

Glistening mosaic tiles on the purely *Modernista* frontage of Antiga Casa Figueres on the Rambla

quality, acorn-fed product is questionable (since Jabugo produces hams of various qualities), and the price for the *flauta* is, frankly, too good to be true. But what is incontrovertible is that the sandwich and the *caña* (draft beer) that goes with it are both excellent. The swinging doors into the kitchen with frosted, acid-engraved glass and the overhead piano balcony combine to make this one of Barcelona's best snackeries.

shop

Shops in the Raval are heavy on textile and jewellery design—a spin-off from the MACBA's artistic influence—though shoe emporiums are also springing up everywhere, especially near the MACBA end of Carrer Elisabets. Shops displaying glass, books, fashions, fine foods and music are accumulating in this increasingly gentrified labyrinth of back streets. Most of the shops in the Raval are between the MACBA and the Rambla (*map p. 22, C3*) on Carrers Bonsuccés and Elisabets (the extension of Bonsuccés), Pintor Fortuny, del Carme, Doctor Dou and Notariat. Shops open and close with some celerity here, so be prepared for hot new emporiums not listed here as well as addresses that have closed or changed proprietors. All shops are located on map pp. 22 & 23.

On Carrer Elisabets, **Ⓐ Llibreria Central del Raval** bookstore, at no. 6, is housed in what was once the Casa de la Misericòrdia chapel (*see p. 34*). Always a breath of fresh air and an inspiration to go and read somewhere, the Central del Raval has vaulted ceilings harking back to the monastic peace and quiet that once reigned here. A few steps farther down on Carrer del Notariat is **Ⓑ Terranyina**, at no. 10, a textile studio, shop and school (offering courses as short as two days: ideal for visitors to Barcelona) occupying a lovely space filled with wooden looms under late 19th-century wooden roof beams. Farther down Carrer Elisabets, in Carrer Doctor Dou, is **Ⓒ Transforma**, on your left at no. 16, a multi-purpose designer of furniture, lamps, clothing items,

ceramics and glass. Paco Pérez does lighting, decorating and furniture while Glòria Miralbell is the ceramics and glass specialist. At no. 10 is **Ⓒ Galeria-Llibreria RAS** specialising in books and magazines on art, architecture, design and photography. The store design by Jaime Salazar neatly connects with the gallery's main theme. Back on Carrer Elisabets, three shops in a row **Ⓐ** (**Twiggy**, **Boba** ● and **Vialis**) all share an address: Carrer Elisabets 20. Twiggy and Vialis sell shoes by preponderantly Barcelona designers, though some of them have come from afar (such as Chie Mihara from Japan). Boba shows women's clothing designed by the hot Barcelona design team of Giménez y Zuazo. **Ⓐ Bhuno**, at no. 18, shows and sells clothing items by Confaldasyaloloco, Who, Hergenhahn and Jocomomola, as well as items designed by store owner Barbara Oliveras. Ahead, past the Camper hotel is the shoe shop **D Camper** at Plaça dels Àngels 4, with graffiti-covered walls and a wide variety of funky shoes anarchically displayed all over the room. The Camper store is called a 'Walk in Progress', meaning that they are occupying that space until the owners and designers come up with a better idea, so the shop may not be here by the time this book prints. Around the corner at Carrer dels Àngels 8, **D Espai Vidre** is all about glass, space in which to admire, study, research and buy a wide range of this ancient yet innovative material. **D The Air Shop,** at no. 20, displays lamps, paintings, dresses, cushions, poofs, vases, curtains and an ever-growing chaotic enumeration of inflatable objects, handy and easily packed gifts for travellers. The art gallery downstairs holds exhibits with arts and crafts based on the use of air.

Other addresses to seek out: **E The Buffet&Ambigú** book and utensil store hidden away in the Passatge 1800 offers an infinity of books and miscellaneous artefacts for the food-obsessed. Specialised cooking gear includes goggles for tear-free onion peeling, contraptions for making foam of spaghetti, olive oil sprayers and kitchen blowtorches. **F El Indio**, just down Carrer del Carme at no. 24, is an old-fashioned textile cutting house with reams of materials to cut on lengthy wooden tables. The Art Nouveau details on the façade include acid engravings in the glass and looping parabolic hyperboloid-shaped door handles. Just off the Rambla, **G Xocolater Bellart** at Carrer del Carme 3 makes artisanal chocolate in a shop good enough to eat (look up for the ceiling painting and the rich chocolate *Modernista* woodworking dating from the store's 1890 founding).

H Etnomusic at Carrer Bonsuccés 6, behind a lovely 18th-century storefront announcing *estereria* (basket weaving), has music from all over the world, including Arabic flamenco, Tibetan temple bells, tantric harmonics, dolphin songs, and belly dancing. The **I Casa Beethoven** music store tucked into a corner next to the Palau Virreina (*see p. 28*) at La Rambla 97 is one of Barcelona's most revered traditional spots for finding musical equipment, scores and instruments. Dating from 1880, the shop behind the *Modernista-Noucentista* façade stocks more than 100,000 musical scores and books approaching 99% of the world's available materials. Other music-related curios and bric-a-brac range from musical neckties and key chains to music boxes and (of course) busts of Beethoven.

GOTHIC
QUARTER

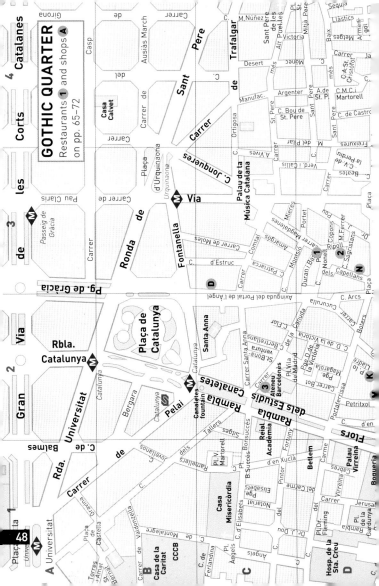

GOTHIC QUARTER

Restaurants **1** and shops **A**
on pp. 65–72

4 les Corts Catalanes

3

2

1

48

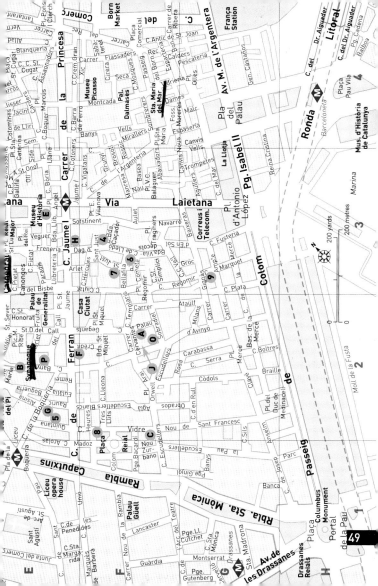

introduction

The Gothic quarter is a warren of medieval streets clustered around the cathedral on the hill the Romans called Mons Taber, the Acropolis-like high ground edified in the 1st century BC. The Temple of Augustus occupied the very crest, the site now visible—fluted columns and all—on Carrer Paradís just behind the cathedral. This is the oldest part of Barcelona, with half-hidden vestiges of the ancient Roman colony and proud reminders of medieval prosperity. There is much to explore and peruse within these hushed alleys: the cathedral; the City History Museum's Iberian, Roman and Visigothic underground; the medieval Jewish quarter. But the Barri Gòtic is more than just a monument to the past. In these resonant spaces, often reverberating with the notes of a street musician's guitar or flute, life still goes on. Antiques shops, art galleries, carpenters, furniture restorers, luthiers, chic restaurants, wine bars, cafés, outdoor terraces and a thousand Gothic and neo-Gothic nooks and crannies to browse through make this *rovell d'ou* (the 'yoke of the egg', as the trace of the Roman 1st–4th-century walls has been described) a source of continual discovery.

•The Cathedral

Open: Daily 7.45–1.30 & 4–7.45 **Charges:** Free entry **Metro:** Jaume I **Map:** p. 49, E3
Highlights: Images of Santa Eulàlia; *Pietà* by Bartolomé Bermejo

Popularly known as La Seu, Catalan for 'the seat' (of the Bishopric), Barcelona's Catedral de la Santa Creu i de Santa Eulàlia (Cathedral of the Holy Cross and of Santa Eulàlia) is officially dedicated to the Holy Cross, its highest spire crowned with the figure of St Helen, finder of the True Cross in Jerusalem and mother of Rome's first Christian emperor, Constantine. It is Santa Eulàlia, however, whose tomb is in the crypt, who commands the stronger cult here.

Most of the present building was constructed between 1298 and 1450, though a church has occupied this site since the 3rd century. The neo-Gothic façade and lantern spire were added between 1892 and 1913 by Josep Oriol Mestres, architect of the Liceu opera house (*see p. 29*). The two octagonal bell towers are late 14th-century: the tower on the southern side for tolling ecclesiastical offices from matins to compline; and the other, traditionally used as the city clock tower, for calling citizens to prayer and for ringing curfew.

The interior

[A] Images of Santa Eulàlia:

Barcelona's very own saint was a virtuous virgin born into a wealthy merchant family in the village of Sarrià (still a prosperous area of Barcelona). She was tortured and put to death by Dacian, Roman governor of Tarragona, for refusing to renounce her Christian faith, and was martyred in AD 304. Four scenes showing Eulàlia's torture and martyrdom are sculpted in high relief on the choir screen. From left to right, the first scene shows Dacian attempting to break her faith with flattery, bribery, and, ultimately, torture. Her left hand is on her heart; her right hand points at a cross in the distance. In the next scene Eulàlia is tied to a post and whipped by Dacian's henchmen. In the third scene she is shown having fainted from her wounds. Finally, we see her being

Cathedral

[J]   [I]

[A] Santa Eulàlia images	**[F]** Cloister
[B] Lepanto Chapel	**[G]** Museum
[C] Martorell altarpieces	**[H]** Capella de Santa Llúcia
[D] Tomb of Santa Eulàlia	**[I]** Archdeacon's House
[E] Choir stalls	**[J]** Diocesan Museum

lashed to a saltire (X-shaped) cross in Plaça del Pedró. Tradition says that a fall of snow chastely covered her body until fellow Christians rescued it.
[B] Lepanto Chapel: Contains the *Sant Crist de Lepant*, a 15th-century painted wood sculpture of a dark-skinned Christ. The sculpture was fixed to the bowsprit of the Spanish flagship at the naval battle fought between the Holy League and Ottoman Turkey in the Gulf of Patras off Lepanto (now Nafpaktos, Greece) in 1571 (a life-size model of that ship is housed in the Maritime Museum; *see p. 36*).
[C] Martorell altarpieces: Bernat Martorell, the Catalan medieval

master, produced these narrative altarpieces which are full of detail and pictorial information. His altarpiece of *Saints Cosmas and Damian* is adjacent to the Lepanto Chapel. The chapel of St Benedict, in the ambulatory, has his altarpiece of the *Transfiguration* (1452). Christ stands in the centre with his disciples and Moses and Elijah. On either side are images of the *Transfiguration*, the *Wedding at Cana*, and the *Feeding of the Five Thousand*.

[D] Tomb of Santa Eulàlia: Eulàlia was originally interred in the church of Santa Maria de les Arenes (Saint Mary of the Sands), over which the Santa Maria del Mar basilica (*see p. 76*) was built. Her body was moved to the newly-constructed cathedral crypt in 1339, where it remains to this day, in an elaborate tomb of Italian alabaster supported on eight columns and decorated with scenes from her life. Eulàlia's cult is still very much alive, and her tomb an object of veneration.

[E] Choir stalls: These oaken 15th-century stalls feature misericords carved with predominantly secular scenes ranging from a couple in an amorous pose to the killing of a pig. Also notable are the painted coats of arms on their backrests. In 1519 a convocation of crowned heads of Europe met here to discuss defending the continent against the Ottoman menace. Each delegate was a member of the Order of the Golden Fleece, a chivalric group founded by Philip of Burgundy in 1429; the shields denote where each prince or duke sat during the conference, including Emperor Charles V (Grand Master of the Order), and England's King Henry VIII to the right, facing the altar.

[F] Cloister: A door in the south aisle leads out to the tranquil, shady cloister centred by a tropical garden and pool with 13 pure white geese, one for each of Santa Eulàlia's 13 tortures. Legend has it that these geese are descendants of the flock from Rome's Capitoline Hill. The keystone vault at the centre of the cloister represents Saint George, Barcelona's patron saint, slaying the dragon, as does the bronze sculpture atop the fountain in the eastern corner.

[G] Museum: The most prized possession is a *Pietà* by Bartolomé Bermejo (1490), in which a bespectacled St Jerome, news reporter-like, takes in every detail of events for his

Vulgate Bible. Works by medieval master Jaume Huguet are also on display.

[H] Capella de Santa Llúcia: This corner chapel is dedicated to St Lucy. In order to avoid an offer of marriage, Lucy is said to have mutilated herself by tearing out her eyes, which she then presented to her suitor on a tray, a scene graphically depicted over the altar. St Lucy is patron saint of the blind and partially-sighted, of seamstresses and of spiritual enlightenment.

[I] Casa de l'Ardiaca (Archdeacon's House): Casa de l'Ardiaca now houses the municipal archives (upstairs), while the vestibule reveals the inside of part of the 4th-century Roman walls and a section of the aqueduct that brought water into Roman Barcino from the Collserola hills. The marble letterbox by the entrance was designed in 1895 by Lluís Domènech i Montaner for the Lawyers' Association. It is said that the swallows were intended as symbols of the swiftness of truth and natural justice, while the turtles stand for the plodding pace of legal administrative procedures. Every June, the diminutive courtyard opposite the Santa Llúcia chapel hosts one of the most ornate dancing egg displays in Barcelona. *L'ou com balla*, literally, 'the egg how it dances', involves placing an egg on top of the jets of water from a fountain. The spurt of water, surrounded by elaborate arrangements of flowers and fruit, acts as a natural juggler.

[J] Casa de la Pia Almoina (Diocesan Museum): Formerly a house of charity the museum now displays a collection of religious sculptures, liturgical objects, and a Gaudí video explaining his architectural discourse. The building itself, though much restored, is a good place to study Roman Barcino in the vestibule's detailed scale model of the walled garrison town. Roman stones are visible in the interior of what was the only octagonal watchtower of the 82 that ringed the 4th-century Roman colony (*open Mon–Sat 10–2 & 5–8; Sun 11–2*).

A market occupies the Plaça de la Seu in front of the cathedral on Thursdays. It's a browser's boon and bonanza of antique books and art objects.

Plaça del Rei &
Museu d'Història de la Ciutat

Open: Museum open 1 Jun–30 Sept Tues–Sat 10–8, Sun and holidays 10–3; Oct–May Tues–Sat 10–2 & 4–8, Sun and holidays 10–3; night tours are available in July Mon & Tues 9pm–11.30pm, Aug–Sept Tues & Wed 9pm–11.30pm **Charges:** Entry charge
Tel: 933 151 111 **Metro:** Jaume I **Map:** p. 49, E3
Highlights: *Adoration of the Magi* by Jaume Huguet in the Royal Chapel; Saló del Tinell medieval hall

Plaça del Rei is an elegant, unadorned medieval square once thought to have been the scene of Columbus's return from his voyage to the New World. Ferdinand and Isabella, were famously portrayed receiving 'the Discoverer' in June 1493 on the semi-circular steps at the top of the square, though later evidence placed the King and Queen at a summer residence at Badalona, just up the coast.

The **Palau Reial Major** (Main Royal Palace; *pictured overleaf*) in Plaça del Rei was the official royal residence in Barcelona from the time of the Visigoth Ataulfo in the 5th century until the permanent establishment of Spain's royal court in Madrid in 1560. The entrance to the palace is up the stone stairway. On your left as you enter is the old ceremonial chamber, the **Saló del Tinell**, a magnificently barrel-vaulted banquet hall built in 1362 and nicknamed for the *tinells* (vats) containing the royal grain supply. The windows that originally gave out onto the square are walled up now, lending the hall an even more tenebrous, medieval atmosphere. To the right of the main entrance is the 14th-century **Capella Reial de Santa Àgata** (Royal Chapel of St Agatha), a typically slender-naved Catalan Gothic chapel with a handsome coffered ceiling. Its altarpiece, almost three dimensional in the effect of its gilding, is an *Adoration of the Magi*, painted by medieval master Jaume Huguet in 1465, and is the chapel's main treasure. To the left, don't miss the portrait of Santa Àgata, with the attributes of her martyrdom (her severed breasts) on a plate in her right hand.

The 16th-century **Palau del Lloctinent** (Governor's Palace) possesses window hoods decorated with dozens of tiny sculptures, testimony to late Barcelona's early Renaissance creative and ornamental energy. This palace was inhabited by the governor-general of Catalonia during the 16th and 17th centuries, after the houses of Aragon and Castile joined, and royal power had been transferred to Madrid. Above it looms the dark 15th-century **Torre Mirador del Rei Martí** (King Martin's Watchtower) built by Antoni Carbonell.

The Royal Palace in Plaça del Rei, official royal residence from the 5th century to 1560

The hulking steel sculpture *Topo* (1985), meaning 'space' in Greek, is by the Basque sculptor Eduardo Chillida. It stands at the lower edge of Plaça del Rei, while a tiny shrine to La Mercè, Our Lady of Mercy, Barcelona's other patron saint (alongside Santa Eulàlia), is embedded high in the wall to the left.

Palau Clariana Padellàs, moved to this spot stone by stone from the nearby Carrer Mercaders in the early 20th century, is now the **Museu d'Història de la Ciutat** (City History Museum; *for opening times, see above*). Situated under and around Plaça del Rei, this museum's display follows the development of Barcelona from the first Iberian settlement to Roman and Visigothic times and beyond. The Roman remains are the most fascinating. Vestiges of an entire civilization lie beneath your feet—beautifully preserved mosaic floors of Roman colonists' homes, wine cellars, dyers' workshops—as you wander through and above it all on metal and transparent glass walkways.

Palau de la Música Catalana

Open: Tours daily 10–3.30, except when there is a concert or event in the hall **Entrance:** Carrer del Palau de la Música **Charges:** Entry charge; timed tickets only (English tours on the hour), advance booking is recommended **Tel:** 932 957 200 **Web:** www.palaumusica.org **Metro:** Catalunya, Urquinaona **Map:** p. 48, C3 **Highlights:** Auditorium interior

This *Modernista* tour de force, generally understood to be the flagship of Barcelona Art Nouveau architecture, was designed by Lluís Domènech i Montaner (1905–08), employing the best decorative artists and artisans of the day: sculptors Eusebi Arnau, Miquel Blay and Pau Gargallo; stained glass worker Antoni Rigalt i Blanch; and ceramicist Lluís Bru. The venue was conceived by the openly Catalan nationalist Orfeó Català musical society as a symbol of music at the popular level in response to the aristocratic Liceu opera house (*see p. 29*) on the other side of the Rambla. The Palau and Liceu have traditionally been opposing forces in Barcelona's ongoing musical, social, political, linguistic and ideological debate.

The exterior

Miquel Blay's sculptural group is an allegory of Catalonia's popular music and stands tall over the corner of Carrers Amadeu Vives and Sant Pere Més Alt. National patron St George the dragon-slayer centres the procession while around him are women, children and fishermen all swelling the chorus. For a lifelike detail, look for the little boy peeking fearfully over the balcony rail, or the rolled up *barretina*, the traditional Catalan peasant cap, on the figure to the right of the flowing maiden. At the top of the main façade, above the busts of Palestrina, Bach and Beethoven (with Wagner, in his characteristic Bavarian beret, around the corner to the right) is a ceramic mosaic portrayal of a choral scene, the Orfeó Català in full concert. Over and above everything, barely visible, is a ceramic egg, a symbol of fertility and rebirth much used by the *Modernistes*, adorned with floral motifs, the Catalan colours and the red and white cross of St George.

Recently restored over Blay's corner sculptural group is a seven-foot stainless steel lantern and cupola taken down in the 1950s when its stability was threatened by a combination of rust and high winds. Also newly restored are the eight censers or burners around the top of the façade, planned by Domènech i Montaner to emit yellow and red smoke, the colours of the Catalan *Senyera* (banner).

Lower down at street level are the charismatic polychrome ticket windows which, though intricately attractive, give only a hint of what is to come inside. A modern extension at the back, built in 1982–90 by Oscar Tusquets and Carles Díaz, contains the advance ticket office, a library, dressing rooms and rehearsal rooms as well as a sunny courtyard and welcome overspill from the noisy cafeteria.

The interior

Domènech i Montaner maximised the light in an otherwise cramped site by placing the auditorium on the first floor and making the ground floor a spacious, fluid entrance hall. The Palau's auditorium (*pictured left*) is all clamour and commotion even before the music strikes up. In a tribute to European classical music, Wagnerian cavalry lead the charge from the right side of the stage over a bust of Beethoven framed by classical columns. On the left is Catalonia's own music, represented by Josep Anselm Clavé, whose workers' choruses connected classical music and the proletariat; and by the supple maidens of the song *Flors de Maig* (May Flowers). In the centre of the ceiling a dazzling stained-glass inverted cupola-chandelier cascades towards the audience below. The stage, which is shaped like an apse, turns the Palau into an Orphic temple with *bas-relief* muses playing a series of instruments around the back wall. Daylight concerts are particularly spectacular as both the north and south façades are nearly all glass (this was the first steel and glass curtain-wall building in Spain and one of the first in the world) with brightly coloured garlands and crosses of St George alternating with the yellow and red Catalan colours. In the upper reaches of the hall, winged Pegasus-like horses, sculpted by Eusebi Arnau's disciple Pau Gargallo, and fitted with real leather reins, leap out of the wall over the orchestra.

The auditorium of Palau de la Música Catalana is a symphony of *Modernista* sculpture and design, spearheaded by Domènech i Montaner in 1908

Casa de la Ciutat (*open Mon–Fri 9–8, Sat 10–8, Sun 10–2, guided tours Sat & Sun 10–1.30, free entry, Tel: 934 027 000, Metro: Jaume I, Liceu*). Barcelona's Town Hall, with its mid-18th-century Neoclassical façade, stares impassively across what was once the Roman Forum at the Generalitat de Catalunya, the government seat of Catalonia. On the façade of the Casa de la Ciutat are two large statues: Jaume I el Conqueridor (James I the Conqueror; left), the Catalan sovereign count who took the Balearic Islands from the Moors in 1229 and wrested much of the Mediterranean from pirates, thus launching Catalonia's 14th-century commercial empire. Joan Fivaller (right), *conseller* or chief representative in the city parliament known as the Consell de Cent (Council of One Hundred), founded by Jaume I in 1265. He was most famous for his 1416 protest to King Ferdinand I over the payment of a tax on codfish purchased in Barcelona, possibly the earliest recorded instance of Catalonia's famous and much-stereotyped *tacañeria* (stinginess). When the king died that same year, people said that the Conseller's constant harassment had given him apoplexy, and Fivaller became a hero overnight. Around the corner on Carrer Ciutat is what was originally the main entrance. A heavy Gothic doorway is flanked by several spiky sculptures added in the 18th century. A careful look at the arch over the doorway will reveal how the leftover footage of archway was simply stuck onto the new Neoclassical façade when it was built in 1847. Inside are a dozen erotic sculptures by Pau Gargallo, Frederic Marés, Josep Clará, Aristides Maillol, Josep Maria Subirachs and others. Josep Maria Sert's sepia-toned murals cover the main stairway as well as the Sala de les Croniques where Roger de Flor's legendary campaign in Greece during the 14th century is chronicled. The Saló de Cent (Hall of the One Hundred), meeting place for the proto-democratic Barcelona parliament and a stately hall now used for official city events, is the central chamber. **Map p. 49, F2**

Església de Santa Anna (*open daily 10–2 & 4–7, Sun 11–2, Metro: Catalunya*). Hidden away in an easily overlooked cobblestone courtyard is the 12th-century Santa Anna church, one of Barcelona's four earliest (along with the Marcús and Sant Llàtzer chapels and Sant Pau del Camp; *see p. 38*). While retaining its original hulking Romanesque structure, later additions are in the Gothic style, such as the carved main door added in 1300. The three-belled tower over the main entrance and the cloister filled with orange trees are the church's most interesting features along with the 16th-century sarcophagus of noble Miguel de Boera, captain of the Spanish fleet under Holy Roman Emperor Charles V. Built in the form of a Greek cross, the Santa Anna church has been associated with the banned Order of the Knights Templar whose red Greek cross was allegedly found hidden behind the main altar after the church was burned at the outbreak of the Civil War in 1936. Templar crosses, with their characteristic four equal extremities widening at the ends, are visible on the roof of the Sala Capitular to the right of the apse, directly over the main entrance, and on the sarcophagus suspended from the southeast wall of the church on the way into the cloister. **Map p. 48, C2**

Jewish Quarter & Synagogue (*synagogue open Tues–Sat 11–2 & 4–7; Sun 11–2, multi-lingual guided tours available, entry charge, www.calldebarcelona.org, Metro: Liceu*). Barcelona's medieval Jewish quarter, el Call, flourished between the 9th and 14th centuries until in 1391 anti-semitic violence led to the deaths of more than a thousand Jews in Barcelona. Ten years later, the city's remaining Jews were expelled. The four thousand-strong community was originally tucked in near the seat of power (between Carrers del Call and de Sant Sever; *map p. 49, E2*) where they could be protected and provide critical expertise for Barcelona's sovereign counts: eminent philosophers, physicians, poets, astronomers, mathematicians and economists studied and taught here in what was the only university institution of the time, the Escola Major. Five synagogues, hospitals, schools and public baths thrived in the narrow streets of the Barcelona Call. After the 1391 pogrom, the main synagogue became home to the master mason Marc Safont, who was working on the nearby palaces of Plaça Sant

Hebrew tablet set within a wall of the Jewish quarter, el Call

Jaume. The synagogue's eccentric orientation within the surrounding grid, facing southeast to Jerusalem, is one of its identifying characteristics. The menorah, made of recycled metals by Majorcan sculptor Ferran Aguiló, was given to the synagogue in honour of his ancestors. **Map p. 49, E2**

Plaça Reial (*Metro: Liceu*). Plaça Reial is the lower Rambla's great hub and gathering point. Built in 1848 on the site of a former Capuchin monastery, this Neoclassical space designed by Francesc Daniel Molina was initially conceived as a sister square of the Plaça de Sant Josep, now occupied by the Boqueria market (*see p. 28*). Denizens of Barcelona's underworld and homeless vagabonds share benches and the winter sun with tourists. The apartments behind the ochre façades are becoming fashionable spaces for Barcelona and world celebrities ranging from Nobel Prize-winning novelist Gabriél García Márquez to Barcelona architect and urban planner Oriol Bohigas (co-designer of the Hotel Claris; *see p. 13*), or Pasqual Maragall, former mayor and President of the Generalitat. The central fountain, *Les Tres Gràcies*–The Three Graces, Aglaia (Adornment), Euphrosyne (Joy) and Thalia (Bloom)–stands between two lamp posts designed by a 26 year-old Gaudí in 1878. The spiky branches of the lamp and the winged helmet couldn't be less Gaudí-esque, though the open-mouthed, screaming serpents reassure us that the real Gaudí is in there somewhere. Looking out to the Rambla, two pairs of *putti* silhouetted against the sky at either side of the entrance support the crowned royal escutcheons of León and Castile, in honour of Isabella II, Spain's reigning queen from 1833 to 1868. Underneath are medallions commemorating Iberia's great mariners, explorers and conquistadors: Cortés, Pizarro, Magellan, Elkano and Cisneros. **Map p. 49, F1**

Santa Maria del Pi (*open Mon–Sat 10–1.30 & 4.30–7; Sun 10–1.30, Metro: Liceu*). This church, so-named for the pine tree (*pi*, in Catalan) that stood in what was originally a marshy pocket outside the earliest Roman walls, was begun in 1322 and finally consecrated in 1453. Built at the same time as Santa Maria del Mar (begun in 1329; *see p. 76*) and Monestir de Pedralbes (1326; *see p. 111*), these three early Catalan Gothic sister churches, though sharing common characteristics such as the unity of interior space, purity of form, and simplicity of ornamentation, turned out very differently. Santa Maria del Pi is the most fortress-like of all three, a dark quadrangle penetrated only by the main entryway and the mammoth (especially overlooking the tiny Plaça del Pi) rose window, said

The diminutive but picturesque Plaça del Pi and its namesake pine tree

a/s/e Barcelona

to be the world's largest. To best see the colours of the rose window, have a look from inside the church in the afternoon on a sunny day. The lateral façade of the church, around to the left in Plaça Sant Josep Oriol, bears a plaque dedicated to the fall of portly parish priest José Mestres on 6th April 1806, who slipped off the narrow catwalk circling the outside of the apse. Naturally padded and protected, Mestres survived the fall unhurt, and the event was considered a minor miracle; thus the plaque.

Plaça del Pi fills with the interesting tastes and aromas of a natural-produce market (honeys, cheeses) on Thursdays, while neighbouring Plaça Sant Josep Oriol holds a painter's market every Sunday. **Map p. 49, E2**

Temple of Augustus (*open Mon–Sat 10–2 & 5.30–9.30, free entry, Metro: Liceu*). In the courtyard of the region's hiking club, Centre Excursionista de Catalunya, are the 2,000-year-old columns of one corner of the Roman Temple of Augustus: massive, fluted pillars with Corinthian capitals (*pictured right*). They remain here only because Barcelona's early Christians elected not to build their cathedral over the site of the previous temple. Dedicated to the Roman emperor Caesar Augustus, the temple overlooked and occupied the northwest corner of the Roman Forum, which coincided approximately with today's Plaça Sant Jaume (*map p. 49, E2*). Carrer Paradís here is named for the Roman garden or 'paradise' that was once part of the temple. **Map p. 49, E3**

Vestiges of Barcelona's Roman past: remains of the Temple of Augustus, originally part of the Roman Forum complex

eat

The Gothic quarter offers an ample range of dining options running from traditional Catalan fare to Asian, Basque and various forms, flavours and philosophies of fusion cuisine. Plaça Sant Just (*map p. 49, F3*), Plaça del Pi and neighbouring Plaça Sant Josep Oriol (*map p. 49, E2*) are all well populated with restaurants, bars, cafés and taverns for all tastes. For price categories, see p. 11; all restaurants are located on map pp. 48 & 49.

1 €€€ Nonell, *Plaça Isidre Nonell, Tel: 933 011 378, open daily 1–4 & 8–midnight, Metro: Catalunya, Liceu.* ■ Serving market cuisine based on fresh products from the equidistant and excellent Santa Caterina and Boqueria markets, Nonell specialises in a streamlined and eclectic approach to Mediterranean cooking. Poached eggs with truffles, roast suckling pig (a Madrid favourite done perfectly here), wild turbot with hummus, *civet de ciervo con arándonos y castañas* (venison stew with wild cranberry and chestnuts), or *magret de pato y polenta* (duck breast with polenta) are just a few of the consistently interesting proposals on the menu. The wine list is balanced between labels you may not have heard of but will be glad to get to know and established winners. The excellent service is delivered with wit and humour, as well as in English, if you need it. The outside tables are perfect for breezy nights in the heat of summer.

2 €€€ Shunka, *Carrer Sagristans 5, Tel: 934 124 991, open Tues–Sun 1.30–3.30 & 8.30–11, Metro: Liceu.* Rave reviews have filled this excellent Japanese restaurant just behind the Hotel Colón (*see p. 14*) across from the Cathedral (*see p. 51*). If you reserve with less than a week's notice, you may not find a table. The counter, in any case, is the place to be, though still difficult to reserve. The fresh fish, sushi, sashimi and *calamares* (cuttlefish) are all peerlessly selected and prepared. The *makis de anguila* (eel makis) and *makis de pollo* (chicken makis) are superb. Mediterranean and Japanese cooks and cooking have always had much in common (such as a passion for raw fish) and the Catalano-Nipponese fusion phenomenon happening in Barcelona these days, especially at Shunka, is quietly revolutionising the city's dining.

3 €€ Ateneu Restaurant, *Carrer Canuda 6, Tel: 933 185 238, open Mon 10.30–6.30, Tues–Sat 10.30–11.30,*

Metro: Catalunya. This specialist in country cooking from the volcanic Garrotxa region of northern Catalonia shares space with the Ateneu Barcelonés, Barcelona's literary and cultural organisation. Favourites here include recipes based on trout, duck, goose, rabbit and lamb, often accompanied by the famous *mongetes de Santa Pau* (small white beans from the volcanic soil of the town of Santa Pau). The clean-lined glass and stone dining room in what was once the entryway of the Palau Sabassona is another of Barcelona's new-within-ancient interior design triumphs.

④ **€€ Café de l'Acadèmia**, *Carrer Lledó 1, Tel: 933 198 253, open Mon-Sat 1.30-4.30 & 8.30-11, Metro: Jaume I.* Named for the Acadèmia Reial de Bones Lletres (Royal Academy of Belles Lettres) in the nearby Palau de la Comtessa de Palamós, this sophisticated-rustic space populated with wicker chairs and surrounded by ancient stone walls offers light and streamlined Mediterranean cooking. Tables in the square during spring and summer are frequented by politicians and functionaries from the nearby government buildings, especially for weekday lunches. Have a look into the 12th-century Royal Academy building built into the Roman walls at the end of Carrer Bisbe Cassador.

⑤ **€€ Can Culleretes**, *Carrer Quintana 5, Tel: 933 173 022, open Tues-Sat 1.30-4.30 & 8.30-11, Sun 10-1.30pm, Metro: Catalunya, Liceu.* ■ As Barcelona's oldest restaurant (listed in the Guinness Book of Records) generations of the Manubens and Agut families have kept this unpretentious spot at the forefront of the city's dining options for over two centuries. This comfortable restaurant founded in 1786 is quintessential Barcelona in both décor and culinary offerings. Wooden beams overhead and bright paintings of sea and landscapes on the walls surround two dozen tables served by an apparently inexhaustible pool of descendants of the founding patriarchs. Traditional Catalan specialities such as spinach cannelloni with cod, wild boar stew, or the classic white beans with *Botifarra* sausage are prepared by a fleet of home-trained family chefs.

⑥ **€€ Cometacinc**, *Carrer Cometa 5, Tel: 933 101 558, open Mon-Fri 1pm-1am; Sat-Sun 7pm-1am, Metro: Jaume I.* ■ This stylish place in the Sant Just neighbourhood, an increasingly chic zone of artisans and antiquarians, is a fine example of Barcelona's flair for new-over-old interior design. The 30-foot floor-to-ceiling heavy wooden shutters are a visual feast while the artfully prepared interpretations of old standards, such as the *carpaccio de toro de lidia* (carpaccio of fighting bull) with pesto sauce and pine nuts, are lighter, modern versions of traditional dishes. *Atún a la brasa* (tuna cooked over coals) served in

a/s/e Barcelona

sesame puff pastry with an apricot chutney is a house favourite, as is the *lasagna de verdures* (green vegetable lasagna). The lunch menu here is a license to steal.

7 **€€ Pla**, *Carrer Bellafila 5, Tel: 934 126 552, open daily 6–midnight, Metro: Jaume I.* Another sleek design tavern and restaurant in the ever-improving Sant Just neighbourhood, this split-level restaurant is always candlelit and filled with young couples having a quiet (but not too quiet) time. A minimalist glass over ancient stone, brick and wood design successfully captures a contemporary polish in a traditional setting. The cuisine fits the design: light Mediterranean contemporary. Open late on Friday and Saturday, Pla is a good option after a concert at Palau de la Música Catalana (see p. 57).

8 **€€ La Taxidermista**, *Plaça Reial 8, Tel: 934 124 536, restaurant open 1.30–4 & 8.30–12.30am, tapas available 1pm–1am, Metro: Boqueria.* ▬ Salvador Dalí once purchased 200,000 ants and a stuffed rhinoceros in this former natural-science museum and taxidermy shop. Prizewinning architect and designer of public spaces Beth Galí, wife of Barcelona's famed city planner Oriol Bohigas, designed the interior around the building's steel columns and original beams. Innovative dishes rooted in the canons of traditional Catalan and Mediterranean cuisine range from white tuna with goat's cheese and *escalivada* (braised aubergines and peppers) to *bacalao al vapor con judías* (steamed cod with white beans). The *chupito de espuma de crema catalana* (shot glass of crème brulée foam) is a tongue-in-cheek nod to Ferran Adriá's molecular gastronomy movement (see p. 116). The tables outside on the terrace are a great place for coffee or a tapa on sunny winter days.

9 **€ Agut**, *Carrer Gignàs 16, Tel: 933 151 709, open Mon–Sat 1.30–4 & 8.30–11, Metro: Jaume I, Liceu.* This family operation was founded in 1924 and has remained popular ever since, offering no-nonsense Catalan cooking at manageable prices. Wood panelling and weary-looking landscape paintings surround a primarily local crowd in this comfortable eating house in the lower reaches of the Gothic quarter not far from the waterfront. Catalan specialities such as *espinacs a la catalana* (spinach with raisins and pine nuts) are standards here, as is the *pato silvestre agridulce* (sweet-and-sour wild duck). For dessert, the *crema catalana* (custard with a caramelised sugar carapace on top) and the *mel i mató* (fresh cheese and honey) are masterfully prepared.

shop

Shops are scarce in the streets immediately around the Cathedral, but between the 4th-century Roman walls and the Rambla commerce thrives. Portal de l'Àngel (*map p. 48, C2*) swarms with shoe shoppers and music buyers; Carrers Petritxol and de la Palla (*map p. 48, D2*) are filled with art galleries and antiques shops; Carrers Ferran (*map p. 49, D2*) and Portaferrissa (*map p. 48, D2*) are thick with fashions. All shops are located on map pp. 48 & 49.

A **Antonio de Barnola**, *Carrer Palau 4, Tel: 934 122 214, open Tues–Fri 5–9; Sat 12–2 & 5–9, Metro: Drassanes, Jaume I, Liceu.* Built into the former stables under what was once a noble Gothic quarter townhouse, this gallery attempts to marry different artistic disciplines with interior design and architectural themes. Prestigious architects such as Javier Barba Corsini, Michael Graves, Carlos Ferrater, Arata Isozaki, Beth Galí and Enric Miralles have collaborated with the gallery since its founding in 1990. In addition, artists with architectural subject matter have also shown work here, including sculptors such as Sergi Aguilar (with his structural creations) and Lluís Hortalà (with the use of construction materials).

B **L'Arca de L'Àvia**, *Banys Nous 20, Tel: 933 021 598, open Mon–Fri 10–2 & 5–8; Sat 11–2, Metro: Liceu.* The 'grandmother's trunk', as the name of the store implies, is filled with diverse yesterday's items,

from period clothing of the 1920s or 1950s to Art Nouveau curtains and bedspreads to shoes and gloves or hats and hairpins. Far from a flea market, however, L'Arca stocks a whole host of serious antiques, so be prepared to hear some large numbers bruited about when push comes to price.

C **Art Escudellers**, *Carrer Escudellers 12 & 23–35 & Rambla 96, Tel: 934 126 801, open Mon–Sat 10–10; Sun 10–4.30, Metro: Liceu.* In Catalan, an *escudella* is an earthenware pot and the artisans who make them are *escudellers*, so this is the perfect address for a ceramics specialist. Ceramics from all over the Iberian Peninsula are collected in these three locales. The home store at Carrer Escudellers 23–25 offers the best selection of over 140 different artisans from every corner of Spain. Maps showing what part of Spain the work is from are displayed with the ceramics, which range from tiny curios and souvenirs to important works of ceramic artisanship.

D **Casas**, *Portal de l'Àngel 40, Tel: 933 021 112, open Mon–Sat 10am–9pm, Metro: Catalunya.* Homegrown and cosmopolitan shoe designers share space at this easy-to-be-in multi-level shoe emporium at the Plaça Catalunya end of Portal de l'Àngel's melée of shops, mega-shops and boutiques. With their 'Eleven' line of men's shoes, the 'Camila' line for women, and the 'Camelot' for children, there is a funky shoe here for everyone.

E **Cereria Subirà**, *Baixada Llibreteria 7, Tel: 933 152 606, open*

The captivating interior of Cereria Subirà, in business since 1761

Mon–Fri 9–1.30 & 4.30–8; Sat 9–1.30, Metro: Jaume I. Universally famed as Barcelona's oldest shop, open since 1761 (though it was not always a candle store), this *cereria* (chandlery) offers over a thousand types of candles in all sizes, shapes, scents, colours and designs ranging from votive candles to animals and wild mushrooms. Jordi Subirà, master chandler and president of Catalonia's chandlery guild is now combining his craft with Barcelona's passion for design in new creations by young designers. The store's gilded curving staircase and torch-bearing maidens, well worth admiring in their own right (*pictured left*), date from the store's early era as a luxurious textile emporium.

F **Custo Barcelona**, *Carrer Ferran 36, Tel: 933 426 698, open Mon–Sat 10–10; Sun 12–8, Metro: Jaume I, Liceu.* You'll see plenty of Custo outlets around town, but this is the main shop in the Gothic quarter. Once a major international success with clingy cotton tops in vivid colours, the brothers Custo have jumped aggressively into denims, shoes and accessories and are likely to continue on through just about anything the human body can wear, walk on or carry.

G **El Ingenio**, *Carrer Raurich 6, Tel: 933 177 138, open Mon–Sat 10–1.30 & 4.30–8, Metro: Catalunya, Liceu.* Behind this handsome traditional storefront dating from 1838, as the bronze plaque on the pavement outside confirms, are a thousand tricks and baubles ranging from carnival costumes and masks to plastic fruits and veg, ersatz insects, nail-through-hand jokes, sneezing powders and just about everything you could possibly need to liven up life around home.

H Formatgeria La Seu, *Carrer Dagueria 16, Tel: 934 126 548, open Tues–Sat 10–2 & 5–8; Sat 10–3.30 & 5–8, Metro: Jaume I*. The Gothic quarter's best cheese-tasting shop, on the site of an ancient buttery with the 19th-century churn sitting idle in the back room, is the realm and reign of Scotswoman Katherine McLaughlin. Carefully selected artisan-produced cheeses from cow, goat and sheep's milk from all over Spain as well as superb olive oils can be tasted or taken home in Katherine's artistic wrapping paper fashioned from local newspapers. For on-premises tasting, don't miss a chance to use the cheese boards with slots for holding wine glasses.

I Ganiveteria Roca, *Plaça del Pi 3, Tel: 933 021 241, open Mon–Sat 10–1.30 & 4.30–8, Metro: Catalunya, Liceu*. In medieval times, Barcelona was famous for the quality of its sword manufacturers, and this knife and utensil shop is the direct heir to this tradition. Scalpels, switchblades, daggers, pocket-knives, razors, scissors, hatchets, axes, swords, nail clippers, tweezers and penknives are all on display (*pictured right*). Facing the enormous stained glass rose window of

the Santa Maria del Pi church (*see p. 62*), the shop has been on the cutting edge of things for nearly 100 years. Don't miss the city's earliest *sgraffito* designs on the façade overhead.

B Heritage, *Banys Nous 14, Tel: 933 178 515, open Mon–Sat 9.30–1.30 & 4–7.30, Metro: Liceu*. One of the most gorgeous antique storefronts in the Gothic quarter provides the perfect introduction to a quirky miscellany of retro-styles and vintage clothing. Balenciaga, Yves Saint Laurent and the Pertegaz labels are among the famous clothing designers whose creations adorn this elegant haberdashery.

J La Manual Alpargatera, *Carrer Avinyó 7, Tel: 933 010 172, open Mon–Fri 9.30–1.30 & 4.30–8; Sat 10–8, Metro: Catalunya, Liceu*. Run by a sweet team of *avias* (grandmothers) this long-famous boutique has artisans putting together sandals in the back of the showroom where you can watch them work. La Manual has sold handmade rope-sole sandals to everyone up to and including the Pope. Espadrilles such as the model used for dancing the *sardana* (a regional dance with ancient origins where participants dance in circles) are available here, along with custom made creations you can design yourself and have shipped home.

K Molsa—Nou i Vell, *Plaça Sant Josep Oriol 1, Tel: 933 023 103, open Mon–Sat 10–1.30 & 4.30–7, Metro: Liceu*. Next to the Santa Maria del

Pi church (*see p. 62*), this longtime ceramics favourite is easy to overlook amidst all the other action going on in and around this lively part of the city. With, as the name suggests, both old and new pieces on sale, you might find anything from a unique antique tile to a new line of plates, bowls, cups or cooking vessels stacked in this colourful and well-located ceramics shop.

L Oro Líquido, *Carrer de la Palla 8, Tel: 933 022 980, open Mon–Sat 10–1.30 & 4.30–8, Metro: Liceu.* A produce star specialising, as the shop's name suggests, in what the Spanish consider pure liquid gold: olive oils and products derived from

olives from Spain's two dozen olive oil producing regions. Olive oil shaving cream, olive oil lip balm, olive oil soap, olive oil candles along with extra virgin olive oils served up in bottles and canisters that look as if they could contain single malt Scotch whisky, suggest the reverence and respect this treasured Mediterranean staple inspires.

E Papirum, *Baixada de la Llibreteria 2, Tel: 933 105 242, open Mon–Fri 10–8.30; Sat 5–8.30, Metro: Jaume I, Liceu.* Hand-printed wrapping paper, marbled blank books, greeting cards, notebooks, pens and pencils of all shapes and sizes:

One of the sharp displays at knife and utensil shop Ganiveteria Roca

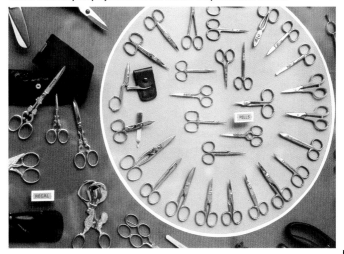

this small specialist has everything you will ever need in the way of materials to write with, in or on. In the middle of the Gothic quarter, Papirum occupies a space that has been at the centre of city commerce and human traffic for over 2,000 years.

M Sala Parés, *Carrer Petritxol 5, Tel: 933 187 020, open Mon 4–8; Tues-Sat 10.30–2 & 4–8; Sun 11.30–2, Metro: Catalunya, Liceu.* A stroll around the wood-panelled floor of the main showroom here is much more than a visual treat: there is an unmistakable redolence of oil paint and three centuries of art and history. Barcelona's oldest operating art gallery, Sala Parés has exhibited every Barcelona artist of note since it opened in 1878. Pablo Picasso and Joan Miró showed here, as did *Modernista* painters Ramon Casas and Santiago Rusiñol before them, and Impressionists Isidre Nonell and Jose María Vidal-Quadras before them.

N S'avarca de Menorca, *Carrer Capellans 2, Tel: 933 425 738, open Mon-Sat 10.30–2 & 5–8.30, Metro: Catalunya, Liceu.* Frequently referred to as *avarcas*, these hand-made leather shoes and sandals from the Balearic Islands come in an infinite range of colours and styles. Based on the traditional homemade calfskin shoes worn by Menorcan farmers, *avarcas* were conceived as strong-soled yet flexible and light footwear for working and walking on rocky and uneven terrain. Different models come with thicker soles for city walking, lighter soles for wearing around the house, or in decorated party models.

O Sita Murt, *Carrer Avinyó 18, Tel: 933 010 006, open Mon–Sat 10.30–8.30, Metro: Jaume I, Liceu.* In the centre of the Gothic quarter, this intricately designed space, with its exposed brick walls and spiral staircase, shows local Catalan and Spanish clothing designers from Julie Sohn to Anna Pianura or the Sita Murt home label. Loose and ample lines and fabrics, and gauzy tops typify this popular, young line of clothing.

P Sombrereria Obach, *Carrer del Call 2, Tel: 933 184 094, open Mon–Sat 10–1.30 & 4.30–7, Metro: Liceu.* Occupying a wonderful corner of this part of the city, Barcelona's most prestigious shop for men's hats of all kinds (mostly berets and golf caps) is a traditional, no-nonsense store decorated simply with a heavy wooden table for merchandise to rest on and a mirror for self-inspection. Safari hats, fedoras, Raider of the Lost Ark hats, homburgs...step in and try on some headgear.

BORN-RIBERA &
BARCELONETA

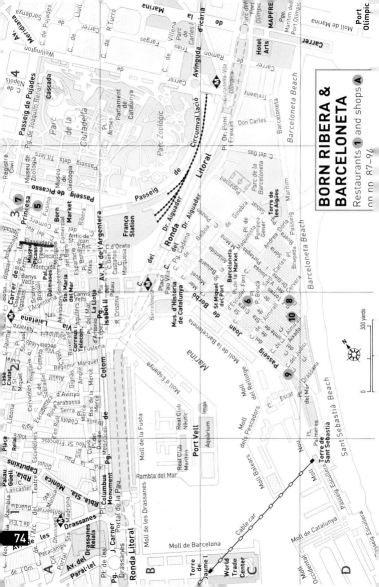

BORN RIBERA & BARCELONETA

Restaurants 1 and shops A
on pp 87–96

introduction

'*Roda el món i torna al Born*' ('Go round the world and return to the Born') was Barcelona's 19th-century way of describing El Born as the centre of the universe, and indeed until the city's main produce market moved out of town in 1971, it was El Born, not the Rambla with its Boqueria market, that generated most of the city's energy. Passeig del Born was the site of medieval jousting tournaments and executions during the Inquisition era, and all processions, carnivals and trade fairs were invariably held here. Today, it is the home of the Picasso Museum and Carrer Montcada, which boasts one noble Renaissance palace after another, the Palau Dalmases, and its lovely courtyard, chief among them.

The old waterfront district of La Ribera is a jumble of narrow streets centred around the church of Santa Maria del Mar. Craft workshops and stylish new bou tiques, lively bars and quiet cobblestone alleyways add up to one of the Ciutat Vella's most atmospheric evening eating and drinking circuits.

Restaurant and shop locations in the Born-Ribera district (see text on pp. 87–89 & 92–94)

Barceloneta, between the harbour and the beach, is the place to come to feel the full blast of the Mediterranean sea air. Long the city's fishing and seafarers' quarter, the district is also home to the gypsy community that produced legendary flamenco dancer Carmen Amaya. Since its regeneration for the 1992 Olympic Games, modern structures now tower above the narrow fishermen's quarters of the 18th century giving Barceloneta a life and look of its own.

Barcelona

a/s/e

● Santa Maria del Mar

Open: Mon–Fri 9–1.30 & 4.30–8; Mass on Sunday at 11, 12.30 & 7.30pm **Charges:** free entry **Metro:** Jaume I **Map:** p.74, A3 **Highlights:** Interior structure

Barcelona's cathedral, La Seu (*see p. 51*), may be the seat of the bishopric, and Gaudí's Sagrada Família (*see p. 99*) the city's most emblematic structure, but the church closest to Barcelona's heart is, beyond a doubt, Santa Maria del Mar (St Mary of the Sea). It was built to protect every element of the Catalan fleet, from sailors and fishermen to ship's chandlers, stevedores and stowaways in fulfilment of a pledge made by Jaume I el Conqueridor (James I the Conqueror) upon capturing Majorca from the Moors in 1229. One hundred years later his great-grandson Alfons III ordered construction to begin. Five centuries later the remains of Barcelona's early patron, Santa Eulàlia, hidden from the Moors in 717, were discovered in an early Christian cemetery on the site of this church, further consolidating the popularity of the seafarers' church.

The most gracefully classical of all Barcelona's churches, Santa Maria del Mar provides a lovely contrast to the ornate architecture of later Gothic, Baroque and—especially—*Modernista* Barcelona. The church was built in a record 54 years (1329-83), by a mere *magister operis* (contractor) stonemason and sculptor named Berenguer de Montagut who carefully selected and shaped each stone brought down one by one from the Montjuïc quarry by the Barcelona stevedores' guild (you can see the small figures of stevedores on the main door). With its symmetry, balance and large areas of masonry without ornamentation, it is the best existing example of early Mediterranean Gothic architecture.

Interior

Anarchist violence in 1936 resulted in the torching of the church, leaving it to burn for 11 days and destroying much inside, including an 18th-century organ and a Baroque high altar as well as a choir stall that took up much of the basilica's now unbroken central space.

a/s/e Barcelona

Structural heights

An engineering feat rather than an architectural vision, the church is an extraordinary example of structural precision. The structure, supported by slender, unarticulated octagonal pillars spreading into a simple rib vaulting, contains relentless symmetry: 16 eight-sided pillars, 2m in diameter, up to 16m from the ground, and another 16m to the keystones. The keystones in turn are 32m from ground level, and the aisles are just 8m lower than the nave. All of these numbers are multiples of, or divisible by, 8: the symbol of the Virgin Mary in medieval mystic numerology. Meanwhile, the nave is exactly twice the width of the aisles; the combined height of the aisles matches the basilica's total width; and the width of the aisles is equal to the difference between their height and that of the nave. The quasi-Pythagorean mathematical balance and proportion suggests the Golden Section or Divine Proportion (A is to B as B is to the sum of A and B); the eurhythmy of Santa Maria del Mar is as seductive to the eye as that of Leonardo da Vinci's drawing of the Vitruvian Man.

Ceiling bosses: These painted bosses represent, from the altar end downwards, the *Coronation of the Virgin*, the *Nativity*, the *Annunciation*, the equestrian figure of King Alfons, who laid the first stone, and the Barcelona coat of arms.

High altar: Against a backdrop of eight pillars, slender and tall as ships' masts, sits a simple statue of the Virgin and Child, with a model of a Barcelona galleon at the Virgin's feet.

St Ignatius step: An engraved stone riser to the left of the north door commemorates the spot where St Ignatius Loyola, founder of the Jesuit Order, begged for alms in 1524 and 1525.

Tombs of the guilds: Laid into the floor are a number of slabs marking the burial vaults of various guilds, stamped with their emblem: a hat for the hatters; a tankard and scales for retailers; a ship in full sail for mariners.

The church is an important music venue in the city and is frequently used for choral events and early music. A concert is highly recommended (details can be found at www.barcelonaturisme.com), as is Midnight Mass on Christmas Eve, if your trip happens to coincide.

Just east of the basilica lies the site of the church's graveyard, **Fossar de les Moreres** (Graveyard of the Mulberry trees). The red marble space is a monument to anti-Bourbon resistance fighters who lost their lives during the siege of 1714. Catalan nationalists still rally here every 11th September to honour their heroic defeat.

The eternal flame on the site of the Fossar de les Moreres for those who fought during the 1714 seige.

a/s/e Barcelona

Museu Picasso

Open: Tues–Sat 10–8, Sun 10–3 **Charges:** Entry charge except 1st
Sun of month **Tel:** 933 196 310 **Web:** www.museupicasso.bcn.es
Metro: Jaume I **Map:** p. 74, A3
Highlights: Childhood works from La Coruña

Housed in three adjoining palaces, the finest of which is the 13th-
century Palau Aguilar with its lovely inner courtyard by the master of
Catalan Gothic, Marc Safont. The museum originated in 1962 on the
suggestion of Picasso's friend Jaume Sabartés, who donated the first
collection of works. Later Picasso himself donated some early works
and in 1981 his widow, Jacqueline Roque, added many more.
Barcelona friends and art gallery owners convinced the Franco-era
mayor, Josep Maria Porcioles, to permit the museum to open; Picasso
was openly hostile to the Generalísimo's regime.

 The Picasso Museum collection doesn't boast a monopoly of the
artist's best paintings, but is nevertheless the world's most comprehensive chronicle of his development. The exhibit is particularly strong on
his early works: the sketches, oils and caricatures from his childhood
years in La Coruña are perhaps the most fascinating part of the museum,
showing the artist's early talent for drawing. These early pieces were
kept at his sister's apartment nearby before being donated to the museum. His *La Primera Comunión* ('First Communion'), painted at the age of
16, gives a clear idea of his youthful mastery of classical painting techniques, as does *Ciencia y Caridad* ('Science and Charity'), where a doctor
and a nun hover around the sickbed of a young mother, pondering
whether either of their ministrations will be sufficient to stave off the
final hour. There are also works from Picasso's blue and rose periods, the
former painted at his studio in the city (at no. 10 Nou de la Rambla;
map p. 23, F3), at that time next door to the salubrious nightclub Eden
Concert. Also shown are the famous 1950s Cubist variations, all 58 of
them, on Velázquez's *Las Meninas*. The drawing *Traginer* ('Carter')
demonstrates Picasso's break with the classical tradition, introducing a
more *Modernista* line, and betraying the influence of Isidre Nonell.

80 *La Primera Comunión* (1896) by Pablo Picasso; an example of his early, more conventional, though masterful, work displayed at the Museu Picasso

Picasso and Barcelona

Pablo Ruiz Picasso spent time in Barcelona between 1895 and 1904. His father was professor at the academy in La Llotja (*see p. 83*) where Picasso, a precocious draughtsman, began advanced classes at the age of 15. At 19 he had his first show at Els Quatre Gats, the famous café which became an exhibition space for Picasso as well as Ramon Casas, Santiago Rusiñol and Isidre Nonell.

Picasso's time in Barcelona, as an impressionable teenager, had much influence on his painting career. It was here that he first saw the work of Isidre Nonell, which helped him break with the orthodoxy of his training up to that time. A year later, it was a show by Ramon Casas at the Sala Parés gallery (*see p. 72*) that caught the 18 year-old artist's eye, and was later reflected in his series of charcoal drawings. Casas was one of the founders of Els Quatre Gats; Picasso began to exhibit there too, and he continued to experiment with different styles. By the time of his second Quatre Gats show in 1900, he had turned himself into a violent Colourist.

Picasso's final two years in Barcelona were dark times for the artist. The early euphoria centred around Els Quatre Gats vanished and the café went bankrupt in 1903. His *Terrats de Barcelona* ('Rooftops of Barcelona'; 1903) portrays a forlorn roofscape of condemned buildings soon to be torn down in the Barri de la Ribera, an area where he and a number of his artist friends lived and had their studios. In 1904 Picasso moved definitively to Paris, where the artistic soil was more fertile. After his move he returned occasionally to Barcelona until his last visit in the summer of 1934. Following the Civil War, being staunchly anti-Franco, Picasso refused to return to Spain. In turn, the Franco regime allowed no Picasso work to be publicly displayed until 1961, when the artist's *sardana* frieze on the façade of Plaça Nova's Guild of Architects building (*map p. 48, D3*) was unveiled. Years later Picasso donated many works to the city he considered his true alma mater.

in the area

Born market (*open Tues–Sat 10–7; Sun 10–2.30, Metro: Jaume I*). The great iron hangar which covers the Born market was designed in 1874 and modelled after Les Halles in Paris. When the market moved out of the district in 1971, La Boqueria on the Rambla (*see p. 28*) took over as the city's central purveyor of fresh produce, and the site became neglected. A project to convert El Born into a public library has recently uncovered remains of this section of the city which was heavily bombarded during the 18th-century War of the Spanish Succession, complete with kitchen fireplaces, tiled floors, wells and the Rec Comtal county canal which brought water into this part of town. Detailed municipal records compiled on the inhabitants have been found which specify who lived in each house, what they did for a living, what they possessed down to the last vat of wine—and even how good the wine was. **Map p. 74, A3**

Carrer Sant Carles No. 6 (*not open to the public, Metro: Barceloneta*). The last original 1755 Barceloneta house left standing, this building was initially planned as a single-family dwelling with work, shop and storage space on the ground floor and the living space above. Overpopulation soon produced split houses and even quartered houses, with workers and their families living in tiny spaces. After nearly a century of living under Madrid-based military jurisdiction prohibiting construction in Barceloneta, homeowners were finally given permission to expand vertically, and houses of as many as five storeys began to tower over the original two-storey structures. **Map p. 74, C2**

Cooperative Obrera La Fraternitat (*open Mon–Fri 10–2 & 3.30–8.30; Sat 10–2, free entry, Tel: 932 253 574, Metro: Barceloneta*). The Workers Co-operative Fraternity is the only Art Nouveau building in Barceloneta, in an otherwise simple and humble fishermen's quarter. Founded in 1879 as a low-cost outlet to help supply workers and their families with basic necessities at cut-rate prices, the co-operative soon became a social and cultural centre that included a public library. The present co-operative building was begun in 1914, opened in 1918, and has now been restored and renovated as, once more, Barceloneta's library. **Map p. 74, C2**

La Llotja (*open Mon–Fri 10–2, Academy of Fine Arts closed Aug, Tel: 933 192 432, Metro: Jaume I*). Barcelona's Llotja de Mar, or maritime trade centre, was one of the main commercial centres of the *Corona de Aragón* the Catalano-Aragonese confederation that dominated Mediterranean trade between the 14th and 17th centuries). It was designed to be the city's finest example of civil architecture. Originally little more than a roof to protect merchants and their wares from the elements, the present building was constructed in the sweeping, wide-arched Catalan Gothic style between 1380 and 1392. At the end of the 18th century the façades were covered in the Neoclassical style of the time, but the interior, the great Saló Gòtic (Gothic Hall; *pictured below*), remained unaltered and was a grand venue for balls and celebrations throughout the 19th century. The Gothic Hall was used as the Barcelona stock exchange until 1975 and, until late 2001, as the grain exchange. The hall has now been brilliantly restored, and though public visits have not been formally established, any chance to see the inside of this historic hall will reveal Gothic arches and columns and a marble floor made of light Carrara and dark Genoese marble, with little windows showing the original Montjuïc sandstone paving tiles underneath. The painted, coffered ceilings, the Neoclassical patio, and the grand stairways are among La Llotja's prime

The Gothic Hall at Barcelona's maritime trade centre, Llotja de Mar

treasures. The **Escola de Belles Arts** (Fine Arts School) occupied the southwestern corner of the Llotja from 1849 until 1960. Many illustrious Barcelona artists studied here, including Gaudí, Miró and Picasso, whose father was an art professor at the school. The **Reial Acadèmia Catalana de Belles Arts de Sant Jordi** (Royal Catalan Academy of Fine Arts of St George) still has its seat in the Llotja, and its museum is one of Barcelona's semi-secret collections of art. Nineteenth-century sculptor Damià Campeny's voluptuous marble sculpture of a moribund Lucretia, on the main floor upstairs to the right, and the young Marià Fortuny's drawings of burly masculine nudes are the collection's stars. **Map p. 74, A2**

Museu d'Història de Catalunya (*open Tues–Sat 10–7, Sun 10–2.30, entry charge except 1st Sun of month, guided tours Sun at noon & 1pm, Tel: 932 254 700, Metro: Barceloneta*). Formerly a warehouse or freight depot, this museum, which opened in 1996, traces 3,000 years of Catalan history from prehistoric times right up to the present day. Exhibit captions are multi-lingual, and many of the displays are interactive and include interesting sections on Romanesque art and Barcelona's trading history. One of the best places to view the harbour and the Mediterranean is from the rooftop cafeteria. **Map p. 74, B2**

Palau Dalmases (*open daily 9–2 & 4.30–7; café open Tues–Sun 7pm–1am, free entry, Metro: Jaume I*). Barcelona's best 17th-century Renaissance patio is showcased here, built into a 15th-century palace. A carved relief of the Rape of Europa runs up the Baroque facade of the elegant stairway cutting across the end of the patio (*pictured right*). Neptune's chariot, cherubic putti, dancers, tritons and myriad musicians accompany Europa's mythological abduction by Zeus, who, in the form of a bull, carries her up the stairs and off to Crete (where she bears him three sons). On either side of the door leading up the stairs are minuscule representations of either *putti*, or maidens covering their nakedness with their arms. These, along with the 15th-century Gothic chapel, with its reliefs of musical angels, and the vaulting in the reception area and main salon, are remnants of the 15th-century palace originally built here. The building is now the seat of the Omnium Cultural, a centre for the diffusion of Catalan culture. Lectures, book presentations and events are open to the public. The Espai Barroc, on the ground floor, is a café with Baroque-era flourishes, period furniture and occasional musical performances. **Map p. 74, A3**

The staircase at the Palau Dalmases showing scenes of the Rape of Europa

Port Olímpic (*Metro: Ciutadella-Vila Olímpica*). Since the athletes departed after the 1992 Olympic Games, the Port Olímpic has turned into a sought-after residential zone with flash buildings towering over the seafront. Most recognisable perhaps is the whale-proportioned goldfish designed by Frank Gehry (1989–92). Here you will also see the marina's twin sky-scrapers: the Hotel Arts (*see p. 12*) and the Mapfre office building looming beside it. Farther left is another Barceloneta landmark, the city's gas company headquarters with its eye-catching cantilever, designed in 1991. It looks over Parc de la Barceloneta with views of the Torre de les Aigües, one of only a few remaining structures from the city's original gas plant. **Map p. 74, D4**

Santa Caterina market (*open Mon 7.30–2; Tues, Weds & Sat 7.30–3.30; Thurs & Fri 7.30am–8.30pm, Metro: Catalunya, Jaume I*). This former 13th-century church and convent became a market in the mid-19th century and developed 'a certain air and aura of a North African souk' according to the late Alexandre Cirici i Pellicer—one of Barcelona's great art and architecture experts. Architect Enric Miralles left behind a revolutionary conception of the marketplace that was executed by his widow, architect Benedetta Tagliabue. From the undulating ceramic mosaic roof with colours and techniques recalling both Gaudí and Miró to the glass floor through which sections of the original convent are visible, this is a unique Barcelona market space. The restaurant cross-references cuisines and ingredients from around the Mediterranean all the way to China and Japan. **Map p. 49, E4**

Sant Miquel del Port (*Metro: Barceloneta*). One of the first buildings to be completed in Barceloneta, this church was begun in 1753 and finished by 1755 under the direction of architect Damià Ribes. Due to strict orders to keep Barceloneta low enough to fire La Ciutadella's cannon over, Sant Miquel del Port had no bell tower and only a small cupola until Elies Rogent added a new one in 1853. This Baroque church has a new version of the winged archangel Michael, complete with sword and chain, in the alcove on the façade. Interesting features include the metopes, palm-size, gilt bas-relief sculptures around the interior cornice and repeated outside at the top of the façade. These 74 Latin-inscribed allegories each allude to different attributes of St Michael: for example, the image of a boat and the inscription *Iam in tuto* (finally in safety), alluding to the protection of St Michael against the perils of the sea. **Map p. 74, C2**

eat

The Born-Ribera district offers a rich variety of restaurants and taverns. Tapas opportunities are everywhere, while bars and nightlife in the tiny streets surrounding Santa Maria del Mar basilica also thrive in this increasingly vibrant shopping and dining hot spot. On the other side of Avinguda Marques de l'Argentera, the beach area of Barceloneta has long been a favourite weekend dining destination, with a dozen good seafood and rice specialists scattered along Passeig Joan de Borbó, along the beach and at the edge of the marina. For price categories, see p. 11; all restaurants are located on map p. 74. For a larger scale map of the Born district, see p. 49.

BORN-RIBERA

1 €€€ El Passadís d'en Pep, *Pla del Palau 2, Tel: 933 101 021, open Tues–Sat 1–4 & 8–11; Sun 1–4, Metro: Jaume I.* A lively bistro which is tucked away through a tiny passageway off the Pla del Palau near the Santa Maria del Mar church (see p. 76). The chefs serve a quick-fire round of delicious seafood tapas and wine as soon as you appear. Sometime later you may be asked to make a decision about your main course, usually fish of one kind or another. Take your pick or stop while the going is good, and graze your way through the rest of this lively area.

2 €€ El Pebre Blau, *Carrer Banys Vells 21, Tel: 933 191 308, open Tues–Sat 1–4 & 8–11; Sun 1–4, Metro: Jaume I.* Age-old wooden doors and shutters surround this space, which offers an ever-self-renewing selection of dishes collected from all over the Mediterranean. Every detail is cared for here with profound taste and judgement, a sybaritic bonanza on the site of the early baths (*banys vells*) of the waterfront district.

3 €€ La Habana Vieja, *Carrer Banys Vells 2, Tel: 932 682 504, open Tues–Sat 1–4 & 8–11; Sun 1–4, Metro: Jaume I.* If you've got a craving for a taste of old Havana—*ropa vieja* (shredded beef) or *moros y cristianos* (black beans and rice) with *mojitos* (a potent but delicious cocktail of rum, mint and sugar) or a round of *plátanos a puñetazos* (punched plantains)—this is the place to come in Barcelona. The upstairs tables overlooking the bar are cozy little crow's nests, and the neighbourhood is filled with quirky dives and saloons for before and after carousing.

Tapas in Barcelona

Tapeo, the ultimate wandering picnic, offers infinite variety and some of the best value eating in the city. Tapas hasn't always been a part of the traditional Catalan menu or way of life, unlike in other parts of Spain such as Galicia or the Basque country. Always on the fringe of matters Iberian, Barcelona has caught up with this miniature cuisine over the last decade or so.

The variety of tapa in Barcelona varies widely. Some of the best bars in the city stick to the beloved simplicity of the potato and ham *bomba* often served with a potent chilli sauce, or *patatas bravas* (crisp, fried potatoes with a 'fierce' tomato sauce) or lightly battered and fried *calamares*. At the other end of the scale, top restaurants influenced and inspired by Ferran Adrià's molecular gastronomy (*see box on p. 116*), are serving ever more innovative miniature haute cuisine in the guise of tapas. Cata 1.81 (*see p. 115*) is producing *brochetas de pollo a la plancha con espuma de cebolla confitada* (grilled chicken brochettes with foam of caramelised onion), while Comerç 24 (*see opposite*) has raised the bar with *Kinder* eggs filled with purée of potato and truffles (*pictured below*) and Casa Lucio (*see p. 132*) is experimenting with the contrasting tastes of mango, foie and *ibérico* ham.

Our ■ Recommended tapas options in the Born-Ribera and Barceloneta districts are:

④ Cal Pep, *Plaça de les Olles 8, Tel: 933 107 961, open Tues–Sat 1–4 & 8–midnight; Mon 8–midnight only, Metro: Jaume I.* Genial Josep (Pep) Manubens delivers excellent fresh tapas, cooked across the counter and served piping-hot in an ecstatic environment. Trust Pep on seating; waiting is worth it. Ask for Albariño (a Galician-produced white wine) while you wait for a place at the counter. If he's offering *cigrons* (chick peas) with spinach, served with or without blood sausage, don't miss it.

⑤ Comerç 24, *Carrer Comerç 24, Tel: 933 192 102, open Tues–Sat 1–4 & 8–11; Sun 1–4, Metro: Jaume I.* The original premises for the artist, aesthete and chef Carles Abellan to playfully reinterpret traditional Catalan favourites such as the deconstructed *tortilla de patatas* (potato omelette), or, for dessert, a postmodern version of the traditional after-school snack of chocolate, olive oil,

salt and bread. His newest venture, Tapaç 24 (*see p. 117*), is situated in the upmarket Eixample offering more of the same creative minimalism.

⑥ La Cova Fumada, *Carrer Baluard 56, Tel: 932 214 061, open daily 1–3 & 7–9, Metro: Barceloneta.* A tiny restaurant and tapas favourite that is always busy, especially at lunchtime with local workers, so it's often difficult to get seated. However, it's well worth the standing time: the *bomba*, a potato and ham croquette, is arguably the best in Barceloneta, where the *bomba* was invented.

⑦ Santa Maria, *Carrer Comerç 17, Tel: 933 151 227, open Tues–Sat 1.30–3.30 & 8.30–12.30am, Metro: Jaume I.* Graduates from Ferran Adrià's unofficial school of cooking (his restaurant El Bulli on the Costa Brava coast) serve up hip miniature delights here with clearly discernable flair, from frogs' legs to coca-cola pudding with pop rocks.

BARCELONETA

⑧ €€€ Andaira, *Vila Joiosa 52–54, Tel: 932 210 007, open Tues–Sat 1–4 & 8–11; Sun 1–4, Metro: Barceloneta.* ▬ New flavours and innovative, contemporary cooking distinguish this young couple's contribution to the Barceloneta dining panorama. It's not that Andaira doesn't do the traditional waterfront rice and fish dishes, but that they do them with a sleek, modern flair, all within sight of the Mediterranean.

€€€ Lluçanès, *Barceloneta market* (**map p. 74, C3**), *Plaça de la Font 1, Tel: 932 242 525, open Tues–Sat 1–4 & 8–11; Sun 1–4, Metro: Barceloneta.* ▬ Chefs and entrepreneurs Àngel Pascual and Francesc Miralles opened two restaurants in the newly renovated Barceloneta market in March 2007. The upstairs gourmet option, Lluçanès, is the award-winning restaurant that moved to town from the remote Osona village of Prat de Lluçanès. Downstairs is the more popular Els Fogons de la Barceloneta, serving typical Barceloneta tapas and seafood specialities. Upstairs look for refined interpretations such as the scallop tartare with white summer truffles from Aragon. Downstairs is more *calamares a la plancha* (grilled cuttlefish) country.

⑨ €€€ Suquet de l'Almirall, *Passeig Joan de Borbó 65, Tel: 932 216 233, open Tues–Sat 1–4 & 8–11; Sun 1–4, Metro: Barceloneta.* ▬ Summer dining is done on an inti-mate terrace outside at Suquet de l'Almirall (the Admiral's Fish Stew), widely regarded as the premier seafood place in Barceloneta (not that the claim is undisputed). Rice dishes from paella to *arròs a banda* (shellfish and rice in fish stock) and *caldoso de bogavante*, a brothy rice dish with lobster, not to mention a fresh *llenguado a la planxa* (grilled sole) all vie for your attention here.

€€€ Torre d'Altamar, *Torre de San Sebastián* (**map p. 74, D1**), *Tel: 932 210 007, open Tues–Sat 1–4 & 8–11; Sun 1–4, Metro: Barceloneta.* The seafood doesn't disappoint here, neither does the variety, however, it is the spectacular views from the dining room which you really want to come to Torre d'Altamar for. Located in the San Sebastián cable-car tower on the waterfront you can view uninterrupted scenes of both the city and the Mediterranean while you dine.

⑩ €€ Can Majó, *Almirall Aixada 23, Tel: 932 215 455, open Tues–Sat 1–4 & 8–11; Sun 1–4, Metro: Barceloneta.* ▬ When the old waterfront *chiringuito* (shack) restaurants along the beach were ploughed under by European Economic Community order in 1992, Can Majó emerged as the most favoured beachfront seafood restaurant left standing. Whether outside on the terrace or in the yacht-like interior dining room, house specialities remain *caldero de bogavante* (a cross

Barceloneta's fishing origins depicted in ceramic tiles

between paella and lobster bouillabaisse) and *suquet* (fish stewed in its own juices). Appetizers from *xipirons* (baby squid) to a plate of *jamón ibérico de bellota* (acorn-fed *ibérico* ham) are standard starters.

9 € Can Manel la Puda, *Passeig Joan de Borbó 60, Tel: 932 215 013, open Tues–Sat 1–4 & 7–11; Sun 1–4, Metro: Barceloneta*. The best choice for a top-value paella in the afternoon sun, Can Manel is near the end of the main road out to the Barceloneta beach. Any time before 4 o'clock is in time for late lunch service. *Arròs a banda* (rice with peeled shellfish) and *paella marinera* (with seafood) or *fideuá*

(with noodles) are all delicious here and a paella for two feeds three without a whimper.

9 € La Mar Salada, *Passeig Joan de Borbó 58, Tel: 932 212 127, open Wed–Mon 1–4 & 8–11; closed Tues, Metro: Barceloneta*. Next door to the often overbooked Can Manel la Puda, this little seafood and rice restaurant with a sunny terrace does creditable paella, black rice, *fideuá*, bouillabaisse, and fresh fish roasted, stewed or *a la sal* (roasted in salt). A local Penedès or an Albariño from Galicia's Rias Baixas with a green or mixed salad completes one of Barceloneta's best value dining opportunities.

shop

The Ribera-Born area seems to be producing design and clothing shops like wild mushrooms. Check along Carrer Banys Vells (*map p. 74, A3*) and the narrow Carrer Flassaders (*see box opposite*) for design items, jewellery and fashions. The aromatic Casa Gispert, just behind the Santa Maria del Mar basilica on Carrer Sombrerers (*map p. 74, A3*), is not to be missed, nor is Baraka, the Moroccan goods expert on Carrer Canvis Vells (*map p. 74, A3*). Vila Viniteca up Carrer Agullers near Via Laietana (*map p. 74, A2*) is always an interesting Bacchic browse, while cheese emporium Tot Formatge is a smart and sassy addition to the district. All shops are located on map p. 74. For a larger scale map of the Born district, see p. 49.

A Atalanta Manufactura, *Passeig del Born 10, Tel: 932 683 702, open Tues–Sat 10–8, Metro: Jaume I.* Handpainted and silk-screened shawls and scarves run wild in this skilled artisan's studio and shop. Design your own: special orders are accepted and shipped along.

B Baraka, *Carrer Canvis Vells 2, Tel: 932 684 220, open Tues–Sat 10–8, Metro: Jaume I.* Pre-haggled goods here are generally cheaper (and better quality) than you could bring back from Morocco. The tagines are gorgeous and the straw poofs are stylish, light and reasonably priced.

C La Barcelana—Estudi Tèxtil, *Carrer Brosolí 1, Tel: 933 198 451, open Tues–Sat 10.30–2 & 5.30–8.30, Metro: Jaume I.* Both La Barcelana (*lana* means wool in Spanish) and Estudi Tèxtil share this attractive space on a side street off Carrer Argenteria. The loom in the back of the shop weaves wool products, while arts and crafts are displayed in the front.

D La Botifarreria de Santa Maria, *Carrer Santa Maria 4, Tel: 933 199 784, open Tues–Sat 9.30–2 & 4–7.30, Metro: Jaume I.* The Catalan sausage, *botifarra*, is the main item on offer at this pork merchant next to the church of Santa Maria del Mar. Varieties include sausage stuffed with spinach, asparagus, cider, cinnamon and Cabrales cheese. In addition, it offers excellent cheeses, hams, pâtés and homemade *sobrassadas* (pork pâté with paprika).

E Casa Gispert, *Carrer Sombrerers 23, Tel: 933 197 547, open Tues–Sat 9.30–2 & 4–7.30; Oct–Dec open Mon too, Metro: Jaume I.* This aromatic shop is bursting with teas, coffees, spices, chocolates and nuts. The almond-roasting oven out back,

Carrer Flassaders (*map p. 74, A3; shops open 10–2 & 5–8*)
This tiny street, named for the medieval manufacture of blankets (*flassades*), is probably El Born's most interesting concentration of boutiques, studios, cafés and restaurants.

Starting from Passeig del Born, **Il Tinello** is at Flassaders no. 44, a delicatessen and restaurant and one of the city's best suppliers of Italian food products. Across the street at no. 41 is **Cortana** with its refreshing, gauzy white fashions for women by Majorca-based designer Rosa Esteva. The sliver of a street to the left is Carrer de les Mosques known as Barcelona's narrowest. The moustachioed face carved into the stone overhead is a medieval announcement for a brothel. At no. 42 is **Loisaida** (Lower East Side in Hispanic slang), selling multiple clothing brands and some antiques. At no. 31 is the shoe store **Check-In**, selling Italian brands such as Janet & Janet and Giardini. On the wall across the street is a spectacular Bourbon coat of arms, marking what was the principality's mint until the late 19th century. **Elisa Brunells**, at no. 36, sells jewellery and accessories, while across the street **Lisa Vixell** is a Swedish designer who makes and sells very feminine things for females, mostly dangerous-looking evening wear. On the corner of Carrer de la Cirera is a gorgeous space, presently closed, but when it opens again well worth a browse for the wooden doors and restoration work alone. A probe up Carrer de la Cirera will reveal **Otman**, at no. 4, specialising in blouses, skirts, frocks and belts made in North Africa, with a tearoom in the back where you can refresh yourself with a pot of mint tea. Back out on Carrer Flassaders, the **Mauri** chocolate shop founded in 1840 is at no. 32, while next door is the **Kaveh Abadani** studio making floral sculptures, jewellery and candelabra, often using silicone. **Almacen Marabi**, at no. 30, is a doll artisan making brightly coloured and fanciful *poupées*. The last stop on Carrer Flassaders is, fittingly, the best: **Montiel, Espai Gastronòmic**, at no. 19, offers fine foods and wines from all over the Iberian Peninsula with a menu loaded with good tastes; an ideal place to settle into a late lunch or an early dinner (*open Wed–Sun 12–5 & 8–11.30*).

dating from 1851, is the star element, but don't miss the acid engravings on the office windows or the vintage wooden back door. Casa Gispert also arranges rural stays in an 11th-century farmhouse in Santa Eulàlia de Ronçana, 30km west, where goats, olives and hazelnuts are raised and harvested (www.canburgues.com).

F **Esther Arias**, *Carrer Cotoners 14, Tel: 932 682 494, open Tues–Sat 11–2 & 4.30-8.30, Metro: Jaume I.* An art gallery and workshop in a lovingly restored space not far from the Picasso Museum (*see p. 79*). Esther Arias shows her work, and others', in monthly temporary exhibits.

G **Olive**, *Plaça de les Olles 2, Tel: 933 105 883, open Mon–Sat 10–9, Metro: Jaume I.* Products from all around the Mediterranean, especially those derived from olives—oils, vinegars, tapenades, cosmetics—fill this glassed-in corner on the bottom floor of the splendid Enric Sagnier i Vilavecchia building. Sagnier was the fourth (and by all measures least talented) of the *Modernista* architects after Gaudí, Domènech i Muntaner and Puig i Cadafalch, but this is one of his best buildings, with a handsome corner turret.

H **Tot Formatge**, *Passeig del Born 13, Tel: 933 195 357, open Tues–Sat 9.30-2 & 4-7.30, Metro: Jaume I.* It's not the size that counts in this small shop which squeezes cheeses from all over Spain and the world onto its shelves. Specialising in local Catalan, Spanish and French products, this is the place for the cheese tour of the Iberian Peninsula and across the length of the Pyrenees. The staff can provide captivating explanations of the geographical and social histories behind the way different regions prepare and produce their respective cheeses.

I **Vila Viniteca**, *Carrer Agullers 7, Tel: 932 683 227, open Mon–Sat 8.30-8.30, Metro: Jaume I.* The best wineshop in Barcelona, in between La Llotja (*see p. 83*) and Santa Maria del Mar (*see p. 76*) with tastings, courses, and events whetting your appetite for further investigation. The streamlined family grocer's shop across the street offers exquisite artisanal cheeses ranging from French goat cheese to Extremadura's famous Torta del Casar.

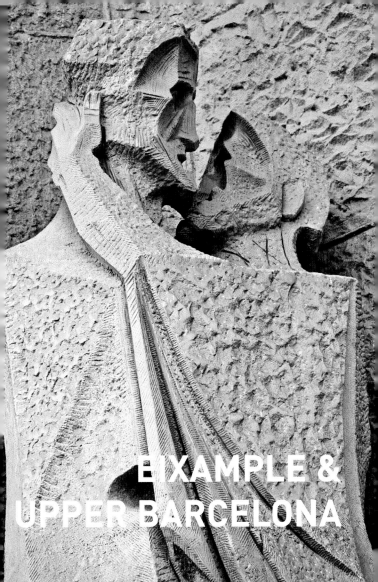

EIXAMPLE &
UPPER BARCELONA

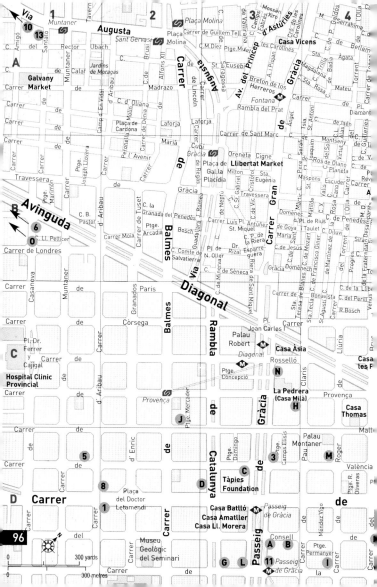

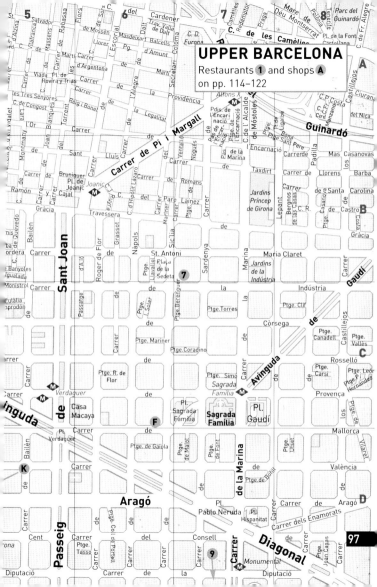

UPPER BARCELONA

Restaurants ① and shops Ⓐ
on pp. 114–122

introduction

Barcelona's Eixample (Expansion) district, Ildefons Cerdà's post-1860 Neoclassical grid, became a showcase for Art Nouveau's extravagant rebuttal to the mechanical uniformity of the industrial revolution. Colour, form and emotion exploded in the streets; straight lines began to writhe. *Modernisme*—Catalonia's interpretation of Art Nouveau—was born. Gaudí began to erect his monument to the Christian faith, the Sagrada Família, amidst the city's new-found industrial prosperity. In a period of only three years (1890-93), known as the '*febre d'or*' ('gold fever') for its headlong stampede of construction, most of the Eixample's early *Modernista* architecture went up. Today the Eixample is a living *Modernisme* museum, with Gaudí's remodelling of Casa Battló, Puig i Cadafalch's Casa Amatller and Domènech i Montaner's Casa Lleó Morera all here. The Eixample is also Barcelona's most elegant shopping preserve.

Upper Barcelona's outlying villages of Gràcia and Sarrià were once separate entities on the far side of the Eixample's grid. There is much Gaudí to explore in upper Barcelona, particularly Park Güell and Casa Vicens, Gaudí's first major commission.

The Pedralbes monastery just above Sarrià is a 14th-century triple-tiered cloister and Clarist convent that ranks among Barcelona's finest sights. With no shortage of shops and restaurants across the upper reaches of Barcelona, Sarrià and Gràcia provide some of the city's best exploring.

a/s/e Barcelona

Sagrada Família

Open: Daily 9–6, May–Oct until 8pm , closed afternoons 25 & 26 Dec, 1 & 2 Jan; guided tours daily at 11.30, 1, 4 & 5.30
Charges: Entrance charge **Web:** www.sagradafamilia.org **Metro:** Sagrada Família **Map:** p. 97, C7
Highlights: Nativity façade by Antoni Gaudí; Passion façade by Josep Maria Subirachs

What George Orwell famously described as 'the ugliest building in the world' has become Barcelona's most universal icon, along with its main architect Antoni Gaudí. Gaudí conceived El Temple Expiatori de la Sagrada Família as nothing less than a three-dimensional representation of the Christian religion: a veritable Bible in stone.

The church was begun in 1882 by Francesc Villar as a grand and solemn undertaking to 'wake faint hearts to faith'. After Villar was dismissed in 1883, the 31-year-old Gaudí was appointed. When asked when the church would be completed, Gaudí's response was always 'My client is not in a hurry'. He worked on the project until his premature death in 1926.

Gaudí planned three façades: those of the Nativity and the Passion are currently complete; an even larger Glory façade will front the main entrance on Carrer Mallorca. Four belltowers will rise over each of the three façades, making a total of twelve, one for each of the Apostles. Around the central Tower of the Saviour will be four larger belltowers, representing the four Evangelists. Another tower in honour of the Virgin will be placed at the west edge of the apse. By 2026, the 100th anniversary of Gaudí's death, after 144 years of construction in the tradition of the early European cathedrals, the Sagrada Família may be officially completed.

[A] The apse: The oldest part of the church, constructed by Villar, resembles a typical 19th-century interpretation of Norman Gothic: solidly built and rather dull. However, Gaudí has made some unmistakable additions: exterior gargoyles in the shape of sea-creatures, lizards, serpents and shells. The apse will ultimately hold 15,000 people, with a choir loft for 1,500, and a total volume

a/s/e Barcelona

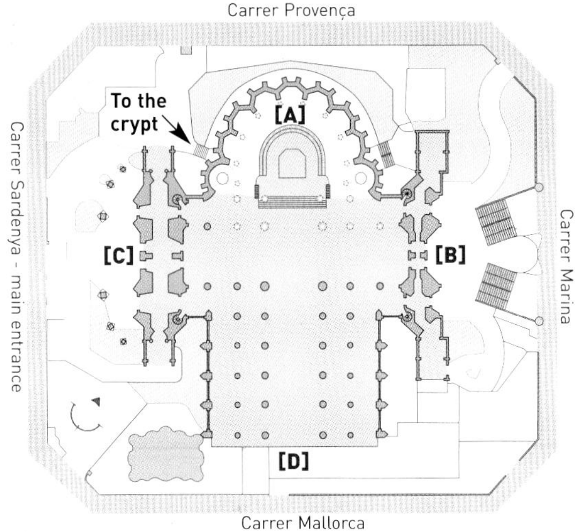

Carrer Provença

Carrer Sardenya - main entrance

Carrer Marina

To the crypt

[A]

[C]

[B]

[D]

Carrer Mallorca

[A] Apse
[B] Nativity façade
[C] Passion façade

[D] Future main entrance
and Glory façade

capable of housing the entire Santa Maria del Mar basilica (*see p. 76*). Below is the crypt where Gaudí's work began with the flowery Art Nouveau capitals. It is also where he is buried.

[B] Nativity façade: This is the most complete example of Gaudí's work: a radically different and ambitious project intended to dazzle beholders with the full power of scriptural revelation. Soaring skyward in intricate levels of carving and sculpture, the Nativity façade is partly made of stone from Montserrat, home of Catalonia's patron saint *La Moreneta*, the Black Virgin. The façade has three doorways, representing the Christian virtues of Faith, on the right, Hope, on the left, and the greatest of the three, Charity, in the centre. The symbolism of the

Doorway of Gaudí's revelatory Nativity façade of the Sagrada Família, begun in 1893, representing the Christian virtue of Charity

Portal of Charity explores the fundamental mystery of Christianity: why does God the Creator become, through Christ, a part of his own creation? The answer, as given in scripture, is that 'God so loved the world that He gave His only begotten Son' to save man from sin and grant him everlasting life. The serpent, crushed by the central column bearing Matthew's genealogy of Jesus, is surrounded by an iron fence, representing man's enslavement by selfishness and evil. The apple in the snake's mouth refers to the banishment from Eden. Above the column is a portrayal of the Nativity itself, then the Annunciation, and above that the Coronation of the Virgin. The evergreen cypress tree is a symbol of eternity, while the white doves in its branches are souls cleansed by the love of Christ and drawn up to eternal life. On the Portal of Faith to the right, above flora and fauna from the Holy Land, we see Jesus preaching at the age of 13 and Zacharias writing to a premonitory John, the name of his son-to-be, John the Baptist. Above, grapes and wheat symbolise the Communion bread and wine, while the eye and hand represent divine providence. The Portal of Hope, on the left, reads from the bottom-most flora and fauna from the Nile up to Herod's massacre of the innocents and the flight of the Holy Family into Egypt. Joseph, with carpenter's tools, gazes at his son under sculptures of Joachim and Anne, parents of Mary, at her marriage to Joseph. The boat and anchor represent the Church,

Detail of the Sagrada Família doors

with the Holy Spirit in the form of a dove, while overhead is a stalagmite-like sandstone needle from the Montserrat massif.

[C] Passion façade: Based on a Gaudí sketch, this is the work of contemporary sculptor Josep Maria Subirachs, who was chosen in 1986 to continue work on this façade. The sculptural style is markedly different from the Nativity façade, unsurprising perhaps, given the two artists' differing attitudes to their subject. Gaudí was a fervent believer; Subirachs a self-confessed atheist. Subirachs, known for the hard-edged hyperrealism of his work, has never imitated Gaudí, and, in fact he twice pays homage to him in the Passion façade: Gaudí appears over the left side of the main entrance making notes or drawings; and the helmeted Roman soldiers are derived from the Gaudí chimneys on the roof of La Pedrera (see p. 107). The Passion façade follows scenes of Christ's last days, grouped in alcoves above the main door and on either side of it. The scenes begin at the left with the Last Supper. To the right is the night vigil in the Garden of Gethsemane and Peter awakening, followed by the kiss of Judas. In front of the main door is Jesus, lashed to a post during his flagellation. To the right of the entryway is a cockerel, and Peter, distraught over his third denial of Christ. Farther to the right, Jesus, crowned with thorns, stands before Pilate, while just above, moving back to the left, is Simon of Cyrene coming to the aid of Christ after his first fall while dragging his cross. Directly left is the mounted centurion lancing the side of the Church, symbol of the body of Christ, with his spear. Above are the soldiers rolling dice for Christ's clothing, and at the top, in the very centre of the façade, is the crucifixion at Golgotha. The moon to the right of the cross refers both to the sudden eclipse-like darkness at the moment of Christ's death and to the full moon of Easter. To the right are Peter and Mary at the sepulchre, Mary under an egg symbolising the resurrection of Christ. At Christ's feet is a figure with a furrowed brow thought to be a self-portrait of Subirachs (the letter 'S' on his right arm and an outsized hand identifying him as a sculptor). The culminating element in the Passion façade is the eight-and-a-half metre gilded representation of the risen Christ.

Manzana de la Discordia

Metro: Passeig de Gràcia **Map:** p. 96, D3
Highlights: Main salon of Casa Batlló; sculpted façades of Casa
Amatller and Casa Lleó Morera

Manzana means both 'city block' and 'apple' in Castilian Spanish. The
nickname, coined by a 19th-century *Vanguardia Española* journalist, on
what must have been a slow day, puns the jealousies aroused by a
Barcelona architectural face-off and the classical myth of the Apple of
Discord (the prize Paris was charged to bestow upon his favourite god-
dess, Aphrodite). This 'city block of discord' is where the three greatest
figures of Barcelona *Modernisme*–
Antoni Gaudí, Josep Puig i Cadafalch
and Lluís Domènech i Montaner–went
head-to-head and hand-to-hand with
three very different, and very important,
buildings: Casa Batlló, Casa Amatller
and Casa Lleó Morera.

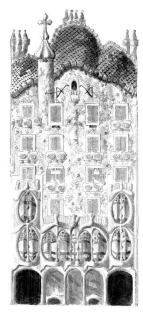

Casa Batlló (*open daily 9–8, entrance
charge, Tel: 934 880 139, www.casabat-
llo.es, Metro: Passeig de Gràcia*). Exotic
and other-worldly, with its rainbow
colouring, mascaron balconies and stip-
pled façade which catches the sunlight
like sequins, Casa Batlló is Gaudí at his
most original. As with much of Gaudí's
work, there is something faintly sinister
about it as well. Gaudí said that he
aimed to create a 'vision of paradise',
though milk and honey seem to have
been replaced with something more hallucinogenic. The entire construct is
imbued with nationalist symbolism.

The undulating roof represents a humpbacked dragon. The turret is St George's lance piercing the monster's side. The ghoulish death's head balconies are supported by the bones of the dragon's victims.

Casa Batlló was a remodelling of an existing building, but Gaudí completely altered the house from inside out. The wavy, sub-aquatic interiors were inspired by Jules Verne's *Twenty Thousand Leagues Under the Sea*, the highlight of which is the swirling roof and aquamarine stained glass in the **main salon**, and the whale-bone structuring of the attic rooms. Another fantastical feature is the intimate inglenook fireplace designed for two in the chimney room. The furniture Gaudí designed for this house is displayed at the Casa-Museu in Park Güell (*see p. 112*).

Casa Amatller (*closed to the public, Tel: 934 880 139, Metro Passeig de Gràcia*). This was the first building of the Manzana de la Discordia to be completed (1900) and was, like Casa Batlló, a remodelling job.

Josep Puig i Cadafalch was the architect chosen by Antoni Amatller i Costa, whose money came from the family chocolate business. Puig i Cadafalch's remodelling is eclectic in spirit, borrowing from the neo-Gothic and Romantic schools, as well as including a Flemish step-gabled roof. The sculptures on the **façade** are by Eusebi Arnau, *Modernisme*'s most celebrated sculptor. Playful animals are shown indulging in Amatller's own pursuits and hobbies. Two rabbits pour liquid chocolate; a pig turns a clay pot while St George and the dragon are locked in combat on the main entrance. The

demure 'Princesa' above is thought to be modelled on Amatller's daughter. In the entryway (well worth seeing) there is an art gallery and a shop specialising in Art Nouveau gifts.

Casa Lleó Morera (*upper floors are closed to the public, lower floors are taken up by the Loewe fashion shop; see p. 121, Metro: Passeig de Gràcia*). The town house that originally stood on this site was extensively remodeled in 1902–06 by Lluís Domènech i Montaner (architect also of Palau de la Música Catalana; *see p. 57*). It was built for Albert Lleó i Morera, and his family, and its avowed aim was to be new and daring: the result is a supreme example both of Catalan *Modernisme* and of the architect's own individual 'floral'

style. The wealth of sculpted decoration swarms across the pinnacle-covered **façade**, and what looks at first like abstract moulding is in fact hundreds of delicate flower motifs. Other decorative elements include female figures using the modern inventions of the age: the telephone, the light bulb, the photographic camera and the gramophone. The main circular balcony makes flamboyant use of the street-corner chamfer.

La Pedrera (Casa Milà)

Open: Daily 10–8, guided tours Mon–Fri 6pm & Sat–Sun 11am; mid-June to mid-Sept the roof is open on Fri & Sat nights for live music, drinks and romantic stargazing **Charges:** Entrance charge **Tel:** 934 845 995 **Metro:** Diagonal, Provença **Map:** p. 96, C3 **Highlights:** Roof and chimney pots

Casa Milà is one of Gaudí's most controversial buildings. It was unveiled in 1910 to the consternation of local residents. Instantly it was dubbed 'La Pedrera' (stone quarry), and the name stuck. Senyora de Milà complained that it looked like a cave for bats and serpents, not a house for human habitation.

Unlike the houses of the Manzana de la Discordia (*see previous page*), La Pedrera was built from scratch on an empty plot, giving Gaudí *carte blanche* to indulge his imagination. The resulting building cost four times its budget, plunging the Milà family into near ruin. Seemingly defying all architectural rules, the exterior has no straight lines and resembles sculpture rather than architecture. Five levels of undulating balconies are bordered by a froth of seaweed-like wrought iron, the work of Josep Maria Jujol (who collaborated with Gaudí at Park Güell; *see p. 112*). The structure has no supporting walls; all the weight is borne by a fretwork of beams and pillars. Gaudí boasted that this made it supremely flexible, convertible for any purpose. The most famous motifs from La Pedrera are from the **roof**, where the twisting **chimney pots** and cowls over the ventilation shafts have been variously interpreted as veiled Scheherazades, Berber nomads, or helmeted warriors. They were nicknamed *espantabruixes* ('witch-scarers') when the building was first unveiled.

To appreciate Gaudí from an engineering perspective, visit the Espai Gaudí in the attic. This has a display of drawings and models explaining Gaudí's theory and practice. On the fourth floor is the Pis de la Pedrera, an apartment-museum that gives a fascinating glimpse into the domestic life of families who once lived here. People—not bats or serpents—still live in the other apartments.

a/s/e Barcelona

Antoni Gaudí (1852–1926)

Few architects have made their imprint on a major city as spectacularly and distinctively as Antoni Gaudí has on Barcelona. His as yet uncompleted Sagrada Família has become emblematic of Barcelona while another dozen works in and around the city continue to draw curious and admiring crowds.

Strictly speaking, and considering his love of decorative detail and his interest in organic forms, Gaudí belongs to the *Modernistes*. In truth his creations have little to do with Art Nouveau: his architecture was revolutionary. He approached construction like no one else before him, dispensing with the circles, triangles and rectangles by which he felt architects had become enslaved. Instead he took his inspiration from the curving lines of nature, and the strength and structural integrity of the organic form. In this lies the secret of Gaudí's genius: he was doing much more than just experimenting with aesthetics; he was putting function before form, and devising an alternative system of construction.

Gaudí's architectural evolution is easy to trace. His first project, Casa Vicens (1883; *see opposite*), is the most conventional, despite its bravura polychrome façade. In essence, it is still a house built of right-angled planes. In Palau Güell (1888; *see p. 30*) the parabolic arch makes its triumphal entrance, though overall Gaudí is still in thrall to the neo-Gothic. With La Pedrera (1906–10; *see previous page*), Gaudí abandons convention more entirely: there are no supporting walls; the structure rests on an inner fretwork of beams. Casa Batlló (1904–06; *see p. 104*), in outward appearance as well as structural concept, is still way ahead of its time. And finally, there is the project that consumed the last 40 years of Gaudí's life, the Sagrada Família (1883–1926; *see p. 99*), more a geological formation than a building, the ultimate experiment in monumental organic architecture, which Gaudí himself once compared to Montserrat, the famous serrated mountain and holy shrine just west of Barcelona.

in the area

Casa de les Punxes (House of the Spikes) (*closed to the public, Metro: Diagonal*). Completed in 1905 for three sisters, this brick-and-stone extravaganza is from Josep Puig i Cadafalch's so-called 'pink period' and clearly demonstrates the architect's interest in northern European architecture. The oriel windows are covered in intricate plateresque decoration, and the six conical turrets would seem more at home in the Black Forest. Today the building consists of private apartments and only the outside can be admired. **Map p. 96, C4**

Casa Vicens (*closed to the public, Metro: Fontana*). This private residence was the 30-year old Gaudí's first important commission, begun in 1883 and completed two years later. The straight lines and angles of the façade—not a parabolic (looping) arch in sight—show that Gaudí was still using the T-square and basing his designs on traditional architectural and engineering canons, embellishing them with extravagant and original touches. The owner, Manuel Vicens, was a ceramics manufacturer, which explains the use of the green and white majolica that gives Barcelona's first polychrome façade its striking appearance. Orientalist themes and Mudéjar motifs give the house many worthy details: the palmetto leaves decorating the gate and surrounding railings by Gaudí's assistant Francesc Berenguer (sections of which have been incorporated into the entrance gate of Park Güell; *see p. 112*); the stylised bats and lizards crawling around the ironwork on the façade. And inside (should the house open to the public), the *trompe l'oeil* birds in the salon, and the Mocárabe, the Moorish stalactite-like carved ceiling in the smoking room. **Map p. 96, A3**

Finca Güell-Pavellons Güell (*open weekdays 9–2, entry charge, Metro: Maria Cristina, Palau Reial*). This little gatehouse to Eusebi Güell's country estate sports one of the most famous Gaudí motifs in the world: the savage wrought-iron dragon, made by the master's own hand. The dragon itself is in chains, with claws outstretched. Originally there was a mechanism by which it would extend its limbs and open the gate. Its eyes were once inlaid with red glass. The park beyond belonged to the Güell family, hence the ornamental letter G on the gate-strut. The gatehouse is now home to

the Càtedra Gaudí, a Gaudí library and study centre open to the public. The former gardens still exist, though much was lost when the final extension of the Diagonal was constructed in 1924. **Map on inside cover**

Monestir de Pedralbes (*open Tues–Sat 10–2, Sun 10–3, Tel: 932 563 434, entry charge except 1st Sun of month, Metro: FGC station Reina Elisenda then a 10-min walk*). Still home to a small community of Clarist nuns, this graceful convent is one of Barcelona's finest off-the-beaten-track treasures. Founded in 1326 by Queen Elisenda, fourth wife of Sovereign Count Jaume II, the convent was dedicated as a home for nuns of the Franciscan order of the Poor Clares, and as a retreat for Reina Elisenda herself when her royal and ancient husband died. Following St Clare's original model, the first community consisted of Reina Elisenda, her mother and sisters, and a handful of women from wealthy families, all living lives of extreme austerity, dependent entirely on alms, and spending their days in devout prayer and meditation. The convent's most famous feature is its cloister (*pictured opposite*), an unusual three-storey structure surrounding a beautiful garden of palms and orange trees. At the entrance, the paving stones have been shattered along shallow grooves: tracks made by French gun carriages when Napoleon turned the nunnery into a barracks during his 1808 occupation of Barcelona. To the right of the entrance is the Cel.la de Sant Miquel, day cell of the Mother Superior, decorated with important murals painted in 1346 by Catalan artist Jaume Ferrer Bassa. The cell is also famous for containing the earliest graffiti in Barcelona. Between the images of St Francis (bearing the stigmata) and St Clare (holding a book and a quill) is a Gothic scrawl that reads 'Joan, no m'oblides' ('John, don't forget me'), a poignant reminder that not all of the novices were deposited in the monastery willingly. You can also visit the nunnery's medieval living quarters, infirmary, wine cellars and refectory, the walls covered with admonitions: 'Silentium! Audi tacens! Considera morientem!' ('Silence! Hear and Hush! Consider that we die!'). **Map on inside cover**

Palau Baró de Quadras (Casa Àsia) (*open Tues–Sat 10–8, Sun 10–2, Tel: 932 387 337, Metro: Diagonal*). Built by the ubiquitous Josep Puig i Cadafalch in 1904 for Baron Quadras, the plateresque (carved in silver-smith-like intricacy) façade of this elegant townhouse-palace comprises the best collection of Eusebi Arnau sculptures in town (other Arnau sites

The peaceful triple-tiered cloister at Monestir de Pedralbes, founded in 1326, with its central garden filled with orange trees and palms

a/s/e   Barcelona

are the façades of the former art café now restaurant, Casa Martí-Els Quatre Gats on Carrer Montsió (*map p. 48, C3*), Casa Amatller (*see p. 105*), Casa Lleó Morera (*see p. 106*), and the marble fireplace at Hotel Espanya (*see p. 37*). One of the best sculptural groups portrays St George slaying the dragon in a vertiginous charge down the façade. The cozy-looking row of alpine chalet-like windows across the top floor suggests that Puig i Cadafalch was still dreaming about northern Europe, as in the Casa de les Punxes across the street (*see p. 109*). Casa Àsia, a cultural and business-related Asian research centre, opened here in 2003. **Map p. 96, C3 Park Güell** (*open daily Nov–March 10–6, April & Oct 10–8, May–Sept 10–9, free entry; Gaudi Casa-Museu open Oct–March 10–6 & April–Sept 10–8, entry charge, Metro: Lesseps, then a 10-min walk uphill or catch Bus 24 to the park entrance*). The idea for Park Güell came from Gaudí's partron Eusebi Güell. Missing the peace and pleasures of a country estate and having admired the Garden City movement on a trip to England, Güell wanted to reinvigorate Barcelona's urban landscape and to position himself prominently within it. The mosaic inscription at the entrance announces 'Park Güell', spelled deliberately in the English manner to emphasize the Anglo-Saxon Garden City concept. Despite all the planning that went into Gaudi and Güell's scheme, no plot of land was ever sold and the Güell family eventually gave the area to the city as a public park. The entrance gate to the park makes use of leftover railing sections taken from the Gaudí-designed Casa Vicens (*see p. 109*). The gingerbread gate-houses are topped with a hallucinogenic red-and-white fly agaric mush-room and a phallus impudicus. The left-hand gatehouse is a bookstore with twisting stairways leading to upper landings while the one on the right is a Park Güell interpretation centre giving a helpful overview of the park. Gaudi's curious mingling of innovative brilliance with naïve infan-tilism is at its most marked here. It is said that when the mother of one of his childhood friends first came to Barcelona and saw his work, she exclaimed that he was 'just doing the same things he always did as a boy'. On the steps ahead is perhaps the most famous motif of the whole park, the patchwork lizard, lolling on the central balustrade. The Hall of a Hundred Columns (there are only 86) at the top of the steps was con-ceived as a covered market for the future community of this garden city. The ceiling is decorated with a collage of *objets trouvés*: fragments of bot-tles, plates, cups and china dolls. Broken pieces of tile, *trencadís*, are assembled as ceiling bosses. Above this hall is the esplanade where Josep Maria Jujol's undulating bench—the most celebrated example of the *tren-*

Josep Maria Jujol's celebrated *trencadís* bench surrounds the esplanade at Park Guell with views over the city to the Mediterranean

cadís technique in the city—borders the *mirador* with superb views towards the Mediterranean (*pictured above*). The Gaudí Casa (now a museum) was designed by Francesc Berenguer and was Gaudí's home for 20 years. It contains furniture from Palau Güell (*see p. 30*), Casa Calvet and Casa Batlló (*see p. 104*) as well as personal objects. **Map on inside cover**

Tàpies Foundation-Casa Montaner i Simó (*open Tues–Sun 10–8, Tel: 934 870 315, Metro: Passeig de Gràcia*). Originally built as the Montaner i Simó publishing house by Lluis Domènech y Montaner in 1886, this was one of the city's first two *Modernista* buildings (the other being Gaudí's Casa Vicens; *see p. 109*). Restored in 1990 by architects Roser Amado and Domènech i Montaner's great-grandson Lluis Domènech, the steel beam-supported façade with Mudéjar motifs now holds the work of contemporary Catalan painter Antoni Tàpies, as well as frequent temporary exhibits. Tàpies, an abstractionist influenced by Surrealism, crowned the façade with his intricate tangle of metal entitled *Núvol i cadira* (Cloud and chair). **Map p. 96, D3**

Barcelona

a/s/e

eat

Dining in the Eixample and upper Barcelona ranges from mid-town chic Drolma to outlying village rustic El Mató de Pedralbes. In between are tapas haunts such as Tapaç 24, contemporary molecular gastronomists Manairó and Cinc Sentits, and specialists at oysters (Gouthier), fin and shellfish (Fishhh!), and authentic Catalan cooking (El Mató de Pedralbes). For price categories, see p. 11; restaurants are located on map pp. 96 & 97, unless otherwise stated.

1 €€€ Can Gaig, *Carrer d'Aragó 214, Tel: 934 291 017, open Mon 8.30–11, Tues–Sat 1.30–3.30 & 8.30–11, Metro: Passeig de Gràcia, Universitat*. This longtime Barcelona favourite continues to dazzle old- and newcomers with carefully prepared traditional Catalan cooking. Perfect cannelloni made with market-fresh ingredients and original combinations balance a menu rich in both maritime and upland specialities, game and domestic raw materials. The *perdiz asada con jamón ibérico* (roast partridge with Iberian ham) or, in season and if available, *becada* (woodcock), in which Carles Gaig is a recognised master, are high in the firmament of star Gaig dishes.

2 €€€ Casa Calvet, *Carrer Casp 48, Tel: 934 124 012, open Mon–Sat 1.30–3.30 & 8.30–11, Metro: Catalunya, Urquinaona*. The former carriage entrance to Antoni Gaudí's Casa Calvet offers a unique chance to dine in an ersatz *Modernista* environment. The dining room features Gaudí-esque ornamentation ranging from looping parabolic door handles to polychrome stained glass partitions, and wood carved in floral and organic motifs. The menu is Mediterranean while the wine list offers a carefully selected choice from all over Spain.

3 €€€ Drolma, *Passeig de Gràcia 70, Tel: 934 967 710, open Mon–Sat 1.30–3.30 & 8.30–11, Metro: Passeig de Gràcia, Provença*. ▪ Inside the Hotel Majestic, Fermin Puig's hyper-refined roost (*pictured opposite*) was an instant success from the day it opened. The seasonally (and almost daily) changing *menú de degustaciò* (taster's menu) might have Scottish grouse cannelloni in foie gras sauce with fresh black truffles in November and December or giant prawn tails with *trompetes de la mort* (black wild mushrooms) and *sot-l'y-laisse* (free-range chicken nuggets) earlier in the autumn.

4 **€€€ Tram-Tram**, *Major de Sarrià 121, Tel: 932 048 518, open Tues–Sat 1.30–3.30 & 8.30–11.30, Metro: Reina Elisenda, Sarrià.* ▪ Tram-Tram is an oasis of refined cuisine. Isidre Soler and his *despampanante* (stunning) wife, Reyes, have put together a fine culinary offering. The constantly changing *menú de degustaciò* might include marinated tuna salad, cod medallions and venison filet mignon. Perfectly sized portions and a streamlined design within this traditional Sarriá house make this a memorable dining experience. **Map on inside cover**

5 **€€ Cata 1.81**, *Carrer Valencia 181, Tel: 933 236 818, open Mon–Sat 6–midnight, Metro: Provença.* ▪ The restaurant's name is taken from the Catalan for wine-tasting, but this little slot is much more than a place to taste wine. With the front piled high with crates and bottles, designer tables soon fill up with delicacies ranging from black truffle omelettes to foie gras. Small plates of exotica such as *tataki de tonyina, sindria caramelitzada, guacamole i daikon* (raw tuna with caramelised melon, guacamole and radish) are also common features at this light morsel specialist.

6 **€€ Fishhh!**, *Avinguda Diagonal 557, Tel: 934 441 139, open Mon–Sat 11–9, Metro: Maria Cristina.* Here you can dine on some top-rate seafood al Lluís Genaro's first-rate fish emporium. Generations of Genaros

The elegant dining room of the Drolma restaurant, part of the Hotel Majestic

Ferran Adrià & Molecular Gastronomy

'Cooking meets science' best describes the essence of molecular gastronomy, a movement which formally came to the table in the early 1990s experimenting with taste, form and cooking methods. Ferran Adrià at his restaurant El Bulli in northern Catalonia and his workshop El Taller in Barcelona entered the culinary spotlight soon after. Originally known as 'the foam guy' for his then radical *espuma de humo* (foam of smoke) creation that captured the aromas of wood smoke in a lighter-than-soufflé montage of air and egg, Adrià went on to give the world rosewater bubbles, Kellogg's Paella (Rice Krispies with sea urchins and a concentrate of prawn heads), and Petrossian caviar tins filled with congealed melon drops. Adrià opened the Pandora's box of culinary creativity and Barcelona's growing fleet of world-famous chefs is basking, to some degree, in his reflected light. Our Recommended ■ restaurants for sampling Barcelona's own molecular gastronomy are (essential to book in advance):

7 **€€€ Alkimia**, *Indústria 79, Tel: 932 076 115, open Mon 1.30–4, Tues–Sat 1.30–3.30 & 8.30–11, Metro: Sagrada Família.*

8 **€€€ Cinc Sentits**, *Carrer Aribau 58, Tel: 933 239 490, open Mon 1.30–4, Tues–Sat 1.30–3.30 & 8.30–11, Metro: Provença.*

9 **€€ Manairó**, *Carrer de la Diputació 424, Tel: 932 310 057, open Tues–Sat 1.30–3.30 & 8.30–11, Metro: Monumental.*

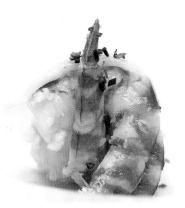

have supplied Barcelona's top restaurants with fine produce from the sea. Genaro and his staff have put together a lively and popular dining space that exudes Boqueria market excitement in the midst of one of the city's busiest shopping venues. **Map on inside cover**

10 €€ Gouthier, *Carrer Mañé i Flaquer 8, Tel: 932 059 969, open Tues–Sat 1.30–3.30 & 8.30–11.30, Sat & Sun 12–3.30, Metro: Sarrià.* Thierry Airaud's attractive, minimalist dining space specialises in oysters, caviars, foies (duck and goose livers) and cavas and Champagnes to go with these exquisite products. Fortunately, the tasting portions allow you to indulge your wildest food fantasies without sustaining massive financial damage. **Map on inside cover**

11 €€ Tapaç 24, *Carrer Diputació 269, Tel: 934 880 977, open Mon–Sat 8am–midnight, Metro: Passeig de Gràcia.* Carles Abellan's most recent culinary venture in Barcelona is a thoroughly hip tapas bar (to complement his first big success, Comerç 24 in El Born; *see p. 89*). The place is usually clogged with at least half a dozen aspiring diners, though if you make it before two o'clock you might find a place at the bar. McFoieburgers (steak topped with duck liver), sizzling iron skillets of *callos* (tripe), and *calçots* (long-stemmed spring onions) with *romesco* sauce and a first-rate wine list make this tapas bar one of the city's best.

● **12 € El Mató de Pedralbes**, *Carrer Obispo Catala, Tel: 932 047 962, open Mon–Fri 1.30–3.30 & 8.30–11.30, Sat 8.30–11.30, Metro: Tres Torres.* ▬ A handy refueling stop after touring the Monestir de Pedralbes (*see p. 111*) named for the *mató* (cottage cheese) traditionally made by the Clarist nuns across the street, this is one of the most authentically Catalan and best-value menus in town. Look for *sopa de ceba gratinée* (onion soup) or *truite de patata i ceba* (potato and onion omelette). **Map on inside cover**

13 € Silvestre, *Carrer de Santaló 101, Tel: 932 414 031, open Mon–Fri 1.30–3.30 & 8.30–11.30, Sat 8.30–11.30, Metro: Muntaner.* ▬ A series of intimate dining rooms and cozy corners are carefully tended by chef Guillermo Casañé and his wife and maître d' Marta Cabot. Fresh market produce from the nearby Mercat Galvany creates *milhojas de calabacín con tomate confitada y queso de cabra* (courgette *millefeuille* with tomato confit and goat cheese) or *colita de rape gratinada con jamón ibérico y cremoso de patatas* (gratineed monkfish fillet with *ibérico* ham and creamed potatoes).

Langoustine tails in a green almond *ajoblanco* soup and almond ice cream, served at the molecular gastronomy specialist Cinc Sentits

shop

Barcelona's Eixample is now universally recognised as one of the world's great shopping environments, a parade of design and fashion shops that could take weeks to explore thoroughly. The Diagonal is lined with fashion emporiums ranging from Adolfo Domínguez to Zara. Vinçon and BD are the chief design stores. Other fertile shopping strips include Carrer Tuset (map p. 96, B2), with a handful of small boutiques. Upper Barcelona's former villages of Gràcia and Sarrià have become shopping neighbourhoods: the factory outlet stores along Carrer Girona could see you shopping 'til you drop. All shops are located on map pp.96 & 97.

Ⓐ Adolfo Domínguez, *Passeig de Gràcia 32 & 89, Tel: 932 720 492, open Mon–Sat 10–10, Sun 12–8, Metro: Catalunya.* One of Barcelona's longtime fashion giants and a leading clothes designer with four shops around town. Recently commissioned to create new uniforms for Iberia Airlines, Adolfo Domínguez has been in the not-too-radical mainstream and forefront of Spanish clothes design for the last quarter of a century. Branches also at Diagonal 490 and Pau Casals 65.

Ⓑ Ágatha Ruiz de la Prada, *Carrer Consell de Cent 314–316, Tel: 934 871 667, open Mon–Sat 10.30–8.30, Metro: Passeig de Gràcia.* Madrid-born, Barcelona-educated design prodigy Ágatha Ruiz de la Prada creates bright-coloured motifs for men, women and children as well as furniture, carpets, ceramics, lamps,

pens, pencils, towels, sheets and even plasters. Miró-like stars, suns, moons, hearts or bright polka dots usually identify Ruiz de la Prada products. A leader of Spain's Green political party, Ms Ruiz de la Prada has been a pioneer in the country's return to European political and artistic leadership since the beginning of Spain's modern democratic era began in 1975 when she was 15 years old. Her bold and colourful designs communicate both humour and a love of nature.

Bagués Joieria, *Passeig de Gràcia 41, Tel: 932 160 174, open Mon–Sat 10am–9pm, Metro: Catalunya.* (**map p. 96, D3**) Bagués has decorated barcelonins since 1839. The Lluís Masriera line of Art Nouveau jewels, intricate flying nymphs and lifelike golden insects, are his most recognisable creations. The location at *Modernista* architect Puig i

Cadafalch's Casa Amatller (see p. 105) is worth the visit just to get a closer look at the house.

BD, *Carrer Mallorca 291–293, Tel: 934 586 909, open Mon–Sat 10–8.30, Metro: Diagonal.* (**map p. 96, C4**) Barcelona Design is a stylish home furnishing store housed in a *Modernista* gem, Lluís Domènech i Montaner's Casa Thomas. Oscar Tusquets, designer and architect, a BD co-founder and author of the new Petit Palau section of Domènech i Montaner's Palau de la Musica Catalana (see p. 57) gives another contemporary design star, Javier Mariscal, plenty of space here, while past giants such as Gaudí, with his Casa Calvet chair, or Salvador Dalí and his Gala loveseat are also available if your pockets are deep enough.

C Bulevard Rosa, *Passeig de Gràcia 53–57, Tel: 932 158 331, open Mon–Sat 9.30–8.30, Metro: Passeig de Gràcia.* This cluster of fashion stores, shoe shops and boutiques of every type is easy to miss if you're not looking for it. Occupying most of the interior of the block, this is your best one-stop shopping opportunity in the Eixample. Boutiques to look for include Tu Tarzán, Yo Jane (no. 85) selling imaginative fashions, and Zambo (no. 39) with an eclectic array of funny looking (but very hip) shoes.

D Colmado Quilez, *Rambla de Catalunya 63, Tel: 932 152 356, open Mon–Sat 10–8, Metro: Diagonal, Provença.* A typical old time Eixample grocers (*colmar* in Castilian Spanish means to 'complete', so grocers at the end of the Eixample blocks became known as *colmados* because they completed the block), this classic space stocks comestibles of every imaginable variety as long as they're exquisite and expensive. Caviars, coffees, wines, cheeses, *ibérico* hams: you can spend an hour just checking out the handsome displays in the window.

E Emporio Santa Maria, *Carrer Casp 57, Tel: 932 478 203, open Mon–Sat 10–8, Metro: Urquinaona.* This quirky store on the corner of Casp and Bailén sells original home decoration wares made by European designers from Holland and Italy. In addition, the Emporio serves lunches from the Mediterranean-Norwegian kitchen of Susannah Taylor (aka Suz): light salads and creative morsels.

F Espardenyes, *Carrer Mallorca 369, Tel: 932 072 049, open Mon–Fri 9.30–1.30 & 4.30–8.30, Sat 10–2, Metro: Sagrada Família.* This excellent little stealth espadrille emporium near the Sagrada Família has managed to pass largely under the radar. Independent from the tourist buzz, prices are aimed at locals and the shop attendants are attentive and helpful.

G Farrutx, *Carrer Diputació 255, Tel: 934 879 314, open Mon–Sat 10–9pm, Metro: Catalunya, Passeig de Gràcia.* Silky soft leather, fragrant as the hills and dales of Mallorca, coupled with chic contemporary design

and painstaking hand-tooled patterns, make this an address to look for in the Eixample's lower reaches.

H Josep Font, *Carrer Provença 304, Tel: 934 872 110, open Mon–Sat 10–9, Metro: Diagonal.* One of the most original and creative designers in Spanish fashion, Josep Font uses colours and textures of neo-Fauvist intensity and proportions to create a line of distinctively romantic apparel for women. One of the few contemporary designers committed to unabashedly feminine (as opposed to feminist) chic, Font lavishes his outfits with ruffles, bows, pleats, pendants and all manner of girlish paraphernalia in a refreshing retreat from the all-important 'edge' that post-modern fashion feels compelled to pursue.

I Julie Sohn, *Carrer Diputació 299, Tel: 934 875 796, open Mon–Sat 10–10, Metro: Passeig de Gràcia.* Expanses of exposed brick walls and a dropped and vaulted ceiling houses Julie Sohn's collections of women's clothing and accessories at her original Carrer Diputació address. Korean-born, Barcelona-based Sohn's clothing combines elegance and edginess, much as the rehabilitated industrial space designed by her husband Conrado Carrasco and his CCT Arquitectos group does with the lines and textures of this handsome space.

J La Central, *Carrer Mallorca 237, Tel: 934 875 018, open Mon–Sat 10–8, Metro: Provença.* La Central, mother ship of La Central del Raval (*see p. 45*), has creaky, literary wooden floors and piles of recent publications with many interesting titles in English. Book presentations here are always interesting events, often with Cava served after the question and answer session.

Loewe, *Passeig de Gràcia 35, Tel: 932 160 400, open Mon–Sat 10–8, Metro: Passeig de Gràcia.* (**map p. 96, D3**) A famous and traditional Barcelona store for men's and women's fashions, Loewe is on the ground floor of one of the three Manzana de la Discordia's famous *Modernista* houses, Casa Lleó Morera (*see p. 106*) by architect Lluís Domènech i Montaner. Loewe is a classic Barcelona clothing and leather emporium, with footwear and accessories of all kinds as well. The Amazona handbag is a classic worth at least having a look at.

K Mantequeria Can Ravell, *Carrer de Aragó 313, Tel: 934 575 114, open Mon–Sat 10–9, Thur & Fri until 11, Metro: Passeig de Gràcia.* The city's top fine food and wine delicatessen and restaurant, Can Ravell is a cult favourite with a peerless supply of just about everything you ever dreamed of sinking your teeth into from Costa Brava anchovies to Basque sheep cheese. Through the kitchen and up a tiny spiral staircase, the dining room offers one of Barcelona's best lunch menus.

Arresting displays inside Barcelona's revered design emporium, Vinçon

Barcelona

a/s/e

Dinners are served on Thursdays and Fridays only. The tasting table downstairs operates on a first-come, first-served basis and brings together foodies from all over the world to swap tastes and tales.

L **Purificación García**, *Passeig de Gràcia 21, Tel: 934 877 292, open Mon–Sat 10–8, Metro: Passeig de Gràcia*. Purificación García enjoys solid prestige in Barcelona as a top guarantee of fashion excellence. A master of fabrics whose creations are rooted in the properties of raw materials, understated hues and subtle combinations of colours and shapes place this contemporary designer at the centre of a new Barcelona aesthetic trend. Other Purificación García locations are at Diagonal 557 and Av. Pau Casals 4.

M **Queviures Murria**, *Carrer de Roger de Llúria 85, Tel: 932 155 789, open Mon–Sat 10–8, Metro: Diagonal*. This historic *Modernista* shop founded in 1890, with colourful windows decorated with Ramon Casas paintings and posters, has an expansive selection of cheeses, sausages, wines and conserves from all over Spain and Europe. The ceramic reproductions of Casas paintings around the interior walls and every detail in this most artistic of grocery stores (*queviures* means 'things to keep you alive') are proof positive that man lives not on bread alone.

N **Vinçon**, *Passeig de Gràcia 96, Tel: 932 156 050, open Mon–Sat 10–8.30, Metro: Diagonal*. With over 50 years at the top of the business, Vinçon's premises take up a rambling *Modernista* house that was once the home of Art Nouveau poet-artist Santiago Rusiñol and the studio of the painter Ramon Casas. It stocks everything from retro furniture to handsome kitchenware (*pictured on previous page*). In amongst the multitude of design elements is a spectacular *Modernista* fireplace designed in wild Art Nouveau exuberance with a gigantic hearth in the form of a stylised face. The back terrace is a cool space with views up to the next-door rooftop warriors of Gaudí's La Pedrera (*see p. 107*).

O **Zapata Joyero**, *Avinguda Diagonal 557, Tel: 934 306 238, open Mon–Sat 10–8, Metro: Provença*. The Zapata family has been an important Barcelona jewellery design and retail operation for over half a century. With original designs and an up-to-date collection of leading Swiss and worldwide watches, this family business is now in its second generation and makes a point of taking good care of clients with large or small jewellery needs. The Zapata store in the L'Illa shopping centre on Avinguda Diagonal specialises in jewellery accessible to smaller budgets.

Barcelona

a/s/e

MONTJUÏC PARK

MONTJUÏC PARK

Restaurants ❶ and shops Ⓐ
on pp. 132–136

124

0   300 yards
0   300 metres

introduction

Montjuïc has a long and varied history, but over the past decade it has become *the* art district of Barcelona. Though long associated with a Jewish cemetery once located here, the name Montjuïc more likely came from the Roman title for this strategic high ground: Mons Jovis, Mountain of Jove or Jupiter. Even before the Romans, the Iberian Barcino tribe occupied Montjuïc, the highest and safest point nearest the sea. From the earliest times, a watch tower was stationed atop the hill and a fortress was first built on the summit in 1640 during the rebellion against Spanish King Felipe IV known as the Guerra dels Segadors (War of the Reapers). The beginning of the 20th century was Montjuïc's cultural hightime when it was singled out as the location for the 1929 International Exhibition, when many of the current halls and pavilions were built. The Palau Nacional now houses the city's main repository of fine art, Museu Nacional d'Art de Catalunya. The Miró Foundation, CaixaFòrum and the Mies van der Rohe pavilion are the other artistic treasures grouped on or around Montjuïc, while the Olympic Stadium, the Palau Sant Jordi sport and mega-concert venue, and the Museu d'Arqueologia de Catalunya complete Montjuïc's cultural offering. Poble Sec is the narrow strip of a neighbourhood tucked in along the northern edge of Montjuïc between Avinguda del Paral.lel and the cliffs of the mountain, and has a handful of notable shops and restaurants.

—Museu Nacional d'Art de Catalunya (MNAC)

Open: Tues–Sat 10–7, Sun 10–2.30, **Charges:** Entry charge **Tel:** 936 220 360 **Web:** www.mnac.es **Metro:** Plaça Espanya **Map:** p. 124, B2
Highlights: *La Batalla de Tetuán* by Marià Fortuny; *Pantocràtor* in the Romanesque collection; *St George and the Princess* by Jaume Huguet

The grandiose domed Palau Nacional, which houses the national museum for Catalonian art, was built as the main pavilion for Barcelona's 1929 International Exhibition. It was originally conceived by Josep Puig i Cadafalch (the exhibition's architect (and designer of Casa Amatller and Casa de les Punxes; *see pp. 105 & 109*). Always controversial, the Palau Nacional was regarded through much of the 20th century as a hodgepodge of over-inflated grandiloquence. When it began literally to fall apart in the late 1970s, many critics called for its demolition. In the end, the Palau Nacional was saved and restored, and its collections expanded. The Romanesque exhibit space was renovated in 1995 by Gae Aulenti (architect of the Musée d'Orsay in Paris) and the Thyssen-Bornemisza and Modern Art collections were moved here in 2004. It was only then that the museum finally became what its name implies: a repository for all Catalan art, covering a thousand years of works.

The Romanesque section is the world's finest collection of early ecclesiastical art, masterminded by Puig i Cadafalch and his teacher Lluís Domènech i Montaner, both experts in early Catalan art. Most of the frescoes were moved from chapels in the Pyrenees during the 1920s, and reproductions put in their place. The 'rock star' (as described by the museum's head curator) of this collection is the **Pantocràtor** from the apse of Sant Climent de Taüll, a strikingly expressive and contemporary representation of Christ in rich colours surrounded by saints, biblical personages and fauna. The Gothic collection contains treasures from Catalonia's medieval zenith, including works by Jaume Huguet (*see box opposite*) and Bernat Martorell.

Gothic glory

Jaume Huguet (c. 1415–92) is one of the best-known painters of the Catalan school. His work had a profound influence on contemporary painting on the Iberian Peninsula. Although he was clearly a medieval painter, with no knowledge of perspective, he went beyond the primitivism of his contemporary Bernat Martorell to invest his work with a deep and touching humanity. More than mere icons, Huguet's paintings show a wealth of detail and everyday observation that give his work the warmth

and intimate appeal that contributed to the classification of his style as Hispano-Flemish. Huguet frequently achieves a three-dimensional effect with embossed metal plates, a technique also seen in his *Epiphany* altarpiece in the chapel of Santa Àgata in the Palau Reial Major (*see p. 55*). His best-known surviving work is his altarpiece of the *Flagellation* (now in the Louvre, Paris). The finest work in the MNAC is his **St George and the Princess** altarpiece (*detail, pictured left*). Other works, notably the *Altarpiece of Saint Augustine*, also appear in the Gothic collection of the museum.

La Vicaria (*The Spanish Wedding*; 1868–69) by Marià Fortuny, showcasing the artist's technical skill for which he became famous, displayed at the MNAC

The Renaissance and Baroque collection features painters such as Ribera, Tiepolo, El Greco, Zurbarán, Francesc Pla 'El Vigatà' and Ceruti. The period between the Gothic and Rococo is covered in the Thyssen-Bornemisza collection with paintings by Rubens, Zurbarán, Tintoretto and Velázquez. The Modern Art collection's star is Marià Fortuny, Spain's most important 19th century painter after Goya, whose stunning battlefield painting **La Batalla de Tetuán** covers an entire wall of room 62. His *L'Odalisca* and *La Vicaria* (*pictured above*) are equally dazzling, revealing his talent for meticulous detail and colouring. Completing this staggering subtreasury of 19th- and early 20th-century artists and sculptors is the Olot school of landscape painters, the leading *Modernista* painters Rusiñol and Casas (whose works here include pencil drawings of Rusiñol and Picasso which hung at the art café Els Quatre Gats), the Catalan Impressionist Isidre Nonell, and a long list of painters from Catalonia and beyond including Boudin, Sisley, Romero de Torres, Regoyos, Sorolla, Zuloaga and Gutiérrez Solana.

Miró Foundation

Open: Tues, Wed, Fri & Sat 10–7, Thurs 10–9.30, Sun 10–2.30
Charges: Entry charge; audioguide recommended **Tel:** 934 439 470
Web: www.bcn.fjmiro.es **Metro:** Plaça Espanya **Map:** p. 124, C3
Highlights: Building by Josep Lluís Sert; *Mercury Fountain* by
Alexander Calder

The permanent collection of the Fundació Miró is a gift from the surrealist painter Joan Miró to his native Barcelona. Born in the Gothic
quarter, Miró also had a studio here until General Franco came to
power, when the artist lived in self-imposed exile, first in Paris and,
after 1956, on the island of Majorca. After Franco's death in 1975,
Miró conceived a project to fill Barcelona with as much of his art as
he could: today his pavement mosaic on the central Rambla (*see
p. 28*), his giant phallic polychrome *Dona i Ocell* ('Woman and Bird')
sculpture in Parc de Joan Miró, and his colourful shooting star *La
Caixa* logo are familiar Barcelona icons.

 The Functionalist building that houses the Miró Foundation was
designed by Miró's personal friend, leading architect and urban planner Josep Lluís Sert. Miró's unmistakable style, filled with playful
colours, Mediterranean sunshine and shadow, is a perfect counter-
weight to the white chromatics and geometrical lines of Sert's architectural idiom. The foundation opened in 1975–almost before Franco
was buried–as a permanent display venue for Miró's paintings and
sculptures, a centre for temporary exhibits, contemporary art studies,
and an archive for scholars and artists. Aside from Miró's own work,
Alexander Calder's 1937 *Mercury Fountain* is the foundation's most
famous work. Calder designed this fountain, which uses actual mercury, for the Spanish Pavilion at the 1937 World's Fair in Paris. It was in
the entrance hall, opposite Picasso's *Guernica*, also commissioned
especially for the exhibition by Pavilion director Sert. Like Picasso's
painting, this sculpture is a political statement, protesting Franco's
siege of the Almadén mercury mines during the Spanish Civil War.

 Joan Miró rests in the cemetery on Montjuïc's southern slopes.

in the area

— **CaixaFòrum (Casaramona)** (*open Tues–Sun 10–8, free entry, Tel: 934 768 600, Metro: Plaça Espanya*). Once a cotton factory and a police barracks, the building is the work of *Modernista* architect Josep Puig i Cadafalch (*see also Casa Amatller and Casa de les Punxes; pp. 105 & 109*). It was reopened in 2002 as a superb arts venue for exhibitions, concerts and other cultural events. The restoration makes full use of ultra-modern design, while respecting the original lines and aesthetic of this redbrick industrial nave. The impressive entryway consisting of two steel trees whose branches support the glass roof of the court-yard was designed by Japanese architect Arata Isozaki, author of the nearby Palau Sant Jordi (*see opposite*). Temporary exhibits and musical events run from September to June; check entertainment listings. **Map p. 124, A2**

Josep Puig i Cadafalch's *Modernista* former factory building, now the restored arts venue CaixaFòrum

— **Castell de Montjuïc** (*open Tues–Sun 9.30–5, entry charge, Tel: 933 298 613, Metro: Paral.lel*). This fortress was built in 1640 during the Catalan uprising known as the War of the Reapers (Guerra dels Segadors), a rebellion against Felipe IV, the poet-king much portrayed by Velázquez. The castle has been repeatedly besieged, most famously in 1705 during the War of the Spanish Succession when Philip of Anjou (subsequently Philip V of Spain) and his forces occupied Barcelona. In 1808, during the Peninsular War, it was

Barcelona

a s/e

seized by the French under Napoleon. During a flare-up of civil unrest in 1842, the city was shelled from its heights for 13 hours by Spanish artillery. The castle presently houses Barcelona's Military Museum (*open Tues–Fri 9.30–6.30, Sat & Sun 9.30–7.30, entry charge*) though rumours abound that when the Barcelona municipal authorities take over the castle, the space may be re-dedicated to a memorial to Republican loyalists executed here during the 1939–75 Franco regime. **Map p. 124, D2–D3**

Estadi Olímpic & Palau Sant Jordi, (*open Tues–Sat 10–2 & 4–7, Tel: 934 262 089, Metro: Plaça Espanya*). The Olympic Stadium was originally built for the 1929 International Exhibition with the idea that Barcelona would then go on to host the 1936 Olympics. Those games were held in Hitler's Berlin instead and Barcelona became embroiled in the outbreak of the Civil War. The city renovated the semi-derelict Olympic stadium in time for the 1992 games, providing seating for 70,000. The Galeria Olímpica museum is dedicated to the history of the Barcelona Olympic movement. An information centre traces the history of the modern Olympics from Athens in 1896 to the present. Just downhill stands the immense **Palau Sant Jordi** sports arena, designed by Japanese master architect Arata Isozaki. The structure, with no pillars or beams to obstruct the view, is famous for having been built from the top down: the roof was built first and then hydraulically jacked into place. **Map p. 124, C1**

Mies van der Rohe Pavilion (*open daily 10–8, entry charge, Tel: 934 234 016, www.miesbcn.com, Metro: Plaça Espanya*). This minimalist structure was created by Ludwig Mies van der Rohe as the German pavilion for the International Exhibition of 1929. Interlocking planes of marble, onyx and glass, a superb architectural template of the Bauhaus School, join reflecting pools to create a shimmering, sleek expanse. Barcelona has traditionally struggled to believe that less could ever really be more—witness the hyper-Art Nouveau Palau de la Música Catalana (*see p. 57*), and the florescent Gaudí spectaculars of Park Güell (*see p. 30*) and Casa Batlló (*see p. 104*). The Pavilion seems no less than a forerunner of Rafael Moneo's Auditori (home to Barcelona's symphony orchestra) and Richard Meier's MACBA (*see p. 33*). Here, economy of line rules. The veins in the green onyx panels are carefully matched, and the black carpet inside the pavilion is deliberately made to mirror itself in the dark water of the pool outside. The interior is minimally furnished with the famous Barcelona chair (also designed by Mies van der Rohe), reproductions of which still grace design-conscious interiors all over the world. **Map p. 124, A2**

eat

Dining on Montjuïc has taken a great leap forward thanks to Oleum, MNAC's excellent restaurant. The Miró Foundation also serves light and delicious lunches. Just off the hill to the north, Poble Sec and the edge of the lower Eixample across Avinguda del Paral.lel offer some good dining opportunities within walking distance of the Montjuïc museums. For price categories, see p. 11. All restaurants are located on map p. 124.

1 **€€ Casa Lucio**, *Carrer Viladomat 59, Tel: 934 244 401, open Tues–Sat 1.30–4 & 8.30–11, Metro: Poble Sec.* ▄ With a small bar in the front room and the encyclopedic Lucio himself to chat with about food and wine while you explore his wife Maribel's creations as they come down the stairs from the kitchen, you're in good hands at this small hideaway just three blocks north of the Paral.lel. Old standards such as *Pochas negras con morcilla* (black beans with blood sausage) or unlikely combinations such as mango, *ibérico* ham and foie gras are likely to find their way onto your plate, accompanied by Lucio's always innovative and interesting wine selections.

€€ Miró Foundation, *Avinguda Miramar 1, Tel: 933 290 768, open Tues–Sat 1–4, Metro: Paral.lel.* For pastas and light Mediterranean fare with exotic touches, Françoise Cauet's stylishly prepared and presented cuisine has an inevitable Gallic delicacy that Joan Miró, who spent two years in Paris after the Spanish Civil War, would no doubt have enjoyed. Goat cheese salads and fresh vegetables accentuate the house predilection for the sleek and streamlined, as if the culinary offerings were imitating the bright planes and clean lines of Josep Lluís Sert's architectural environment. **Map p. 124, C3**

2 **€€ Inòpia**, *Carrer de Tamarit 104, Tel: 934 245 331, open Tues–Sat 7.30–11, Sun 1–4, Metro: Poble Sec.* ▄ Albert, the brother of molecular gastronomist, Ferran Adrià (*see box on p. 116*), shares with his elder sibling a flare for personal warmth and sincerity that the media can't resist. Aside from simplicity and charm, the brothers Adrià can cook. A young, happening crowd packs into this corner tavern just at the edge of the Eixample-Poble Sec border to graze on traditional tapas and small portions of everything from olive samplers in ceramic flutes to Torta del Casar cheeses served in their own wooden mini-crates.

a s/te Barcelona

€€ Oleum, *Palau Nacional,* (**map p. 124, B2**) *Tel: 932 890 679, open Tues–Sun 1–4, Metro: Plaça Espanya.* ■ An elegant and light-drenched space looking out over upper Barcelona and the Collserola hills behind the city, the Palau Nacional (home to Barcelona's national art gallery; *see p. 126*) is a handsome setting for traditional cuisine with contemporary touches. Open for lunch only, the high ceilings and 12-m windows provide a good place to digest the Romanesque exhibit before charging on into the Gothic or the Modern Art collection. In winter you can stretch a lunch of aromatic *raviolis de llebre amb crema de mur-gules* (hare ravioli with wild mushroom sauce) or *"tartaki" de tonyina, cremòs d'avocat i farcellet de verdures en tempura* (tuna tartare with cream of avocado and vegetables in tempura) nearly to sunset, then catch the colourful Magic Fountain music and light show on your way back down the stairs to Plaça Espanya.

3 €€ Quimet & Quimet, *Poeta Cabanyes, Tel: 932 451 164, open Mon–Sat 1–4 & 7.30–10.30, Sat 1–4, Metro: Paral.lel.* ■ A well-kept foodie secret until relatively recently, this tiny but thoroughly enjoyable gourmet haven in Poble Sec is usually too full to find any space in,

La Boqueria market (*see p. 28*) stocks every type of mushroom used in dishes such as *raviolis de llebre amb crema de murgules* (hare ravioli with wild mushroom sauce) at Oleum restaurant (*above*)

but trying it is a good idea anyway. A master *montadito* (canapé) builder, Quimet seems to be able to size up the nature and power of your hunger and thirst and concoct whatever it is you seem to need at any given moment: including excellent cheeses from Catalonia and all over Spain. Everything here comes out of a can or a bottle and will change the way you think about preserved foodstuffs. The wine list is always interesting and Quimet will usually have a suggestion about what would go well with your *montadito*, the relative humidity, or the day's temperature and barometric pressure.

4 **€€ Rosal 34**, *Carrer del Roser 34, Tel: 933 249 046, open Tues–Sat 1.30–4 & 8.30–midnight, Sun 1.30–4, closed Sun evening & Mon, Metro: Paral.lel.* An ancient family wine cellar transformed into a sleek contemporary design space with creative cuisine to match is rivalling neighbourhood gourmet haven Quimet & Quimet (*see above*). Concoctions such as the *patatas allioli y salsa picante* (foam of potato with *allioli* and hot sauce), a potato with *allioli de cuchara* (eaten with a spoon) can be found here. Another signature dish is the *salteado de chipirones de playa con trompetas de la muerte y huevo pochado* (sautéed wild squid with wild mushrooms and poached egg).

5 **€€ Tapioles 53**, *Carrer de Tapioles 53, Tel: 933 292 238, open Mon–Sat 8–11, Metro: Paral.lel.* Sarah Stothart's Mediterranean-Oceania fusion has been a big success in this former Poble Sec umbrella factory turned semi-private restaurant. With a few big tables for groups and a capacity of a couple of dozen diners, you're very much a guest of the house here at this intimate loft-like space.

6 **€ Taverna Can Margarit**, *Carrer de la Concordia 21, Tel: 934 416 723, open Mon–Sat 9–11.30, Metro: Paral.lel.* A unique spot in all of Barcelona for its rustic setting and uproarious service and clientele, this is a fun tavern for simple but delicious cooking in a former stable and wine cellar. Mountainous accumulations of wax conceal candles in the waiting area, while wines flow freely (and for free) from the barrels around the walls. The star dish here is the *conejo a los siete aromas* (rabbit cooked with seven condiments: onion, garlic, thyme, rosemary, cumin, sage and tarragon). The waiters all appear to be brothers and uncles in this family-run restaurant. Order a bottle of cava and you're in for a surprise. Dinner seatings are at 9pm and 11pm only, making reservations essential.

a/s/e Barcelona

shop

Shopping options on and surrounding Montjuïc are centred around the art-themed museum shops at the Museu Nacional d'Art de Catalunya, the Miró Foundation, the Mies van der Rohe Pavilion and CaixaFòrum. Poble Espanyol is the other Montjuïc shopping destination, an architecture village with some 60 artists' and artisans' studios and shops working in textiles, ceramics, glass and leather making everything from jewellery to masks and wedding dresses. All shops are located on map p. 124.

La Botiga CaixaFòrum, *CaixaFòrum* (**map p. 124, A2**), *Tel: 934 768 600, open Tues–Sun 10–8, Metro: Plaça Espanya*. The museum bookstore designed by Pepe Cortés in 2002 has won prizes of its own (the National Design Prize 2006). Rows of suspended lamps illuminate the pot pourri of art-related products on display in this graceful space.

La Botiga del MNAC, *Palau Nacional, Parc de Montjuïc* (**map p. 124, B2**), *Tel: 936 220 360 (ext. 4234), open Tues–Sat 10.15–6.45, Sun 10.15–2.15, Metro: Plaça Espanya*. Beyond the usual offerings of Catalonian art-related souvenirs, mugs, postcards, scarves and general knick-knacks, the 'art à la carte' printing procedure here allows you to take home copies of some 50 of the MNAC's finest works. These high-quality prints represent the only legal way to leave the museum with a Fortuny painting or a fragment of a Romanesque mural.

La Tienda de la Fundació Miró, *Miró Foundation* (**map p. 124, C3**), *Tel: 934 439 495, open Tues, Wed, Fri & Sat 10–7, Thur 10–9.30, Sun 10–2.30, Metro: Plaça Espanya*. T-shirts with Joan Miró's most emblematic paintings, books and guides on Miró and contemporary art in the shop, and an ample miscellany of Miró-related products are on sale in this bright, glass-enclosed space in Josep Lluís Sert's sleek Minimalist building.

Mies van der Rohe Pavilion Shop, *Parc de Montjuïc* (**map p. 124, A2**), *Tel: 934 234 016, open daily 10–8, Metro: Plaça Espanya*. More interesting than the usual assortment of pens, bookmarks and baseball caps with the 'Mies Barcelona' logo is the tabletop-sized scale model of the Pavilion itself or the 'Less is More' t-shirts in black and white. The collection of books and biographies on Mies is more complete than can easily be found elsewhere in the city.

FlorKanela Artesana workshop at the Poble Espanyol craft complex

Ⓐ Poble Espanyol Studios and Shops, *Avinguda Marquès de Comillas s/n, Tel: 935 086 300, open daily 9–6, Metro: Plaça Espanya.* Sixty craft studios and shops occupy gorgeous spaces throughout this architectural park. **Arlequí Màscaras** (no. 106, Casa dels Benavides) makes beautiful coloured masks for all occasions. **Davila-Serra** (no. 77, Casa de los Balbs) is a ceramics and sculpture specialist. **FlorKanela** (no. 86, Casa típica, Montblanc; *pictured above*) is a textile artisan using original looms. **Impronta** (no. 91, Casa típica, Belianes) uses recycled paper to make decorative ornaments, postcards, books and bookmarks. **Luesma Vega** (no. 57, Iglesia de las Carmelitas) is a glass artist making solid glass sculptures in a stunning, high-roofed replica of the Carmelitas church in Alcañiz, Teruel. **Sañudo Artesania en Piel** (no. 78, Casa típica, Santa Pau) makes beautiful and fragrant leather goods from belts to sculptures with traditional leatherworking tools displayed on the studio's back wall. **Aderezo** (no. 38, Casa típica, Morella) is the fashion and design centre of Poble Espanyol, making everything from cocktail dresses to wedding gowns in the latest styles. **Mantones y Mantillas** (no.36, Casa típica, Caldas de Reis) is where Montse Angulo makes handmade Spanish shawls and mantillas for all seasons.

art glossary

Arnau, Eusebi (Eusebi Arnau i Mascort; 1864–1933) *Modernisme*'s leading sculptor whose work is displayed on the façades of Barcelona's best Art Nouveau buildings. Casa Amatller (*see p. 105*), Casa Lleó Morera (*see p. 106*), the Hotel Espanya marble mantelpiece (*see p. 37*), the winged cavalry in the Palau de la Música Catalana (*see p. 57*), and the sculpture at the entrance to the Hospital de Sant Pau (*see p. 36*) are just a few examples of Arnau's work in Barcelona.

Art Nouveau Decorative-art movement which spanned Europe and the US in different guises (as *Jugendstil* in Germany, *Sezessionstil* in Austria, *stile Liberty* in Italy, and *Modernismo* in Spain; *see Modernisme entry*). The style originated in England in the 1880s as a reaction to the bombast of mid-19th century art and the social squalor triggered by the Industrial Revolution. Richly ornamental and asymmetrical with a recurrent whiplash line suggestive of twining plant tendrils, Catalan architects Lluís Domènech i Montaner, Josep Puig i Cadafalch and Antoni Gaudí were the most famous practitioners of Art Nouveau in Barcelona.

Baroque Style of art that dominated the late 17th and 18th century. In Barcelona, Baroque art and architecture is scarce for the same reasons that effected the Renaissance period: economic stagnation and the absence of a royal court (which moved to Madrid in 1560) to stimulate and pay for new works. The Betlem church on the Rambla (*see p. 25*) and Barceloneta's Sant Miquel del Port (*see p. 86*) are some of Barcelona's Baroque buildings. The Casa de la Convalescència and the stairway in Carrer Montcada's Palau Dalmases (*see p. 84*) are the two best Baroque works in Barcelona.

Berenguer i Mestres, Francesc (1866–1914) Architect, close friend and key assistant of Antoni Gaudí on such projects as the Sagrada Família (*see p. 99*) and Park Güell (*see p. 112*). His best known work in Barcelona is the house in which Gaudí lived in Park Güell. When Berenguer died on 8th February 1914, leaving seven children and a widow behind him, Gaudí was deeply affected and said that he had 'lost his right hand'.

Casas, Ramon (Ramon Casas i Carbó; 1866–1932) *Modernisme*'s leading painter studied in Paris with Santiago Rusiñol and Miquel Utrillo. From 1889, Casas exhibited annually at Barcelona's Sala Parés art gallery (*see p. 72*). The public response was initially unenthusiastic, considering his subject-matter flimsy and his palette too restricted. The most famous Casas work is *Garrote vil* (a sketch of which is housed in the Museu Nacional d'Art de Catalunya; *see p. 126*), reflecting the social upheaval of contemporary Barcelona. In 1897, with Rusiñol, Utrillo and Pere Romeu, Casas opened the famous café Els Quatre Gats, a key meeting point for young artists including Picasso. Other works by Casas in Barcelona include the mermaid murals in the Hotel Espanya (*see p. 37*), and the paintings he produced for the Cercle del Liceu, the clubroom of the Liceu opera house (*see p. 29*).

Cerdà, Ildefons (Ildefons Cerdà i Sunyer; 1815–1876) Engineer and urban planner chosen to design Barcelona's post-1860 Eixample district (*map p. 96, C1–97, D8*). Cerdà devised an original plan for a grid of city blocks with interior gardens and chamfered or bevelled corners designed to allow greater light as well as fluid pedestrian and carriage transit through the city. Some of Cerdà's visionary ideas included urban railway lines (as yet unheard-of), a gas supply for (still-uninvented) gas streetlamps, and large-capacity sewers for water storage and flood prevention. Cerdà's plan was ultimately sabotaged, at least in part, by local property speculators who edified the majority of the interior garden areas. Only one of the two planned diagonal avenues was installed, and the Eixample is still inhabited primarily by the well-to-do rather than integrating social classes as Cerdà had envisaged. Throughout his life, Cerdà continued to pursue his vision of creating an urban utopia, gave up a comfortable engineering job to run for parliament, invented the Spanish word 'urbanización' and ran through his family inheritance, dying a semi-pauper and unpaid for his great masterpiece: the Barcelona Eixample.

Corinthian Classical order of architecture from the Greek and Roman era. A major characteristic being capitals decorated with carved leaves. Barcelona's Roman remains contain Corinthian elements, such as the columns of the Temple of Augustus (*see p. 64*).

Domènech i Montaner, Lluís (1850–1924) Barcelona's first *Modernista* architect and a teacher of both Gaudí and Puig i Cadafalch at La Llotja art school (*see p. 83*). At the age of 28, he published a manifesto exhorting Catalan architects to 'search for a national architecture'. His Editorial Montaner i Simó (now the Tàpies Foundation; *see p. 113*) was the first

Modernista building in the Eixample. He built in a distinctive, personal style, using brick, wrought iron and glazed ceramic, with an abundance of floral themes. His best-known works in Barcelona are the Palau de la Música Catalana (*see p. 57*), the Casa Lleó Morera (*see p. 106*), and the Hospital de la Santa Creu i Sant Pau (*see p. 36*). Towards the end of his life he devoted himself to archeology and history and, along with Puig i Cadafalch, was responsible for bringing the unrivalled collection of Romanesque art to what is now the Museu Nacional d'Art de Catalunya (*see p. 126*).

Ferrer Bassa, Jaume (1285–1348) Influenced by the Siena school, by Giotto, he became the best representative of the Italo-Gothic style in Barcelona. His Capella de Sant Miquel chapel murals in the Monestir de Pedralbes (*see p. 111*) are among the city's finest Gothic paintings.

Fortuny, Marià (Marià Fortuny i Marsal; 1838–1874) Recognised as Spain's most important 19th-century painter after Goya. Catalonia's first internationally recognised painter, he was sent to Morocco in 1859 as a pictorial war correspondent. The result was the enormous canvas *La Batalla de Tetuán* (1863) showing the battlefield on which Spain defeated Morocco in 1860. His keen eye for the sensuality of the exotic is reflected in his erotic painting *Odalisque*. A meticulous and highly skilled painter, Fortuny's talents were well used in canvases such as *La Vicaria* or *The Stamp Collector*, where the detail of the interiors is extraordinary, as is the hinted physiognomy of the characters, and the rendering of silk and brocade. Many of his important works can be seen in the Museu Nacional d'Art de Catalunya (*see p. 126*).

Gaudí, Antoni (Antoni Gaudí i Cornet; 1852–1926) Barcelona's iconic architect (*see box on p. 108*), controversial and, for some, an acquired taste. A mediocre architecture student, he had completed only a few small commissions when his work caught the eye of Count Eusebi Güell at the 1878 Paris World Exhibition. Because of that felicitous meeting, Barcelona and Gaudí are now uniquely identified with each other. Whereas Gaudí's work may seem capricious, every detail, no matter how apparently ornamental, is meticulously planned and supremely functional. A wealth of his work can be seen in the Eixample district, including La Pedrera (*see p. 107*) and Casa Batlló (*see p. 104*). His unfinished Sagrada Família church (*see p. 99*) is his ongoing legacy and monument.

Gothic Barcelona's Gothic architecture was built from 14th–16th centuries during the height of Catalonia's prosperity as a Mediterranean commercial empire. Characterised by light, lightness and soaring spaces, Catalan Gothic is, along with *Modernisme*, the city's most emblematic architecture. Curiously, Barcelona's best Gothic buildings are not in the Gothic quarter and include the Ribera's Santa Maria del Mar (*see p. 76*), the Raval's medieval Hospital de la Santa Creu i Sant Pau (*see p. 36*) and upper Barcelona's Monestir de Pedralbes (*see p. 111*). Gothic quarter contributions to the collection are Santa Maria del Pi (*see p. 62*), the spiky later Gothic and neo-Gothic of the Cathedral (*see p. 51*), and the lateral façades of the Town Hall and the Generalitat (*see p. 60*).

Huguet, Jaume (c. 1415–1492) The most representative painter of the Catalan school of the Hispano-Flemish style, which included Bernat Martorell. The elegance of his works and figures communicate a deep melancholy, an artistic break-through at that time (*see box on p. 127*).

Jujol i Gibert, Josep Maria (Josep Maria Jujol i Gibert; 1879–1949) Architect, sculptor and designer, Jujol was a close collaborator of Antoni Gaudí's from 1906, working on La Pedrera (*see p. 107*), whose wrought-iron balconies he designed, and Park Güell (*see p. 112*), where his most famous creation is the undulating bench on the esplanade. Technically talented, Jujol never managed to sustain his early brilliance; his works carried out under the influence of Gaudí were undoubtedly his best.

Martorell, Bernat (1390–1452) Catalan painter and miniaturist, known for his international Gothic style with French-Flemish details. The Museu Nacional d'Art de Catalunya (*see p. 126*) displays his *Martyrdom of Saint Lucy* (1435–40) and his *Altarpiece of Saint Vincent* (1438–40).

Mies van der Rohe, Ludwig (1886–1969) German architect who was a pioneer of modern architecture along with Walter Gropius and Le Corbusier. Following the First World War, Mies and his contemporaries sought a new architecture that expressed the spirit of modern times. He used modern materials such as steel and plate glass for interior spaces, while balancing structural order against the freedom of empty space. He called his structures 'skin and bones' architecture and was known as the inventor of the design aphorism 'less is more'.

Minimalism Architecture stripped down to its barebones indispensable components. Mies van der Rohe's 'less is more' defined his aesthetic of arranging elements of a structure to create extreme simplicity. Everything serves multiple visual and functional purposes (a floor doubles as a radiator, or a reflecting pool is a mirror and light source). Simple surfaces and edges hide unnecessary lines while playing with lighting, geometric shapes and natural textures. Mies van der Rohe's Barcelona Pavilion in Montjuïc Park is the prime example of minimalism in the city (*see p. 131*).

Miró, Joan (1893–1983) Barcelona-born painter, sculptor and ceramicist, Miró was known for a playful, childlike, colourist style that touched an important nerve (or funny bone) in the Catalan zeitgeist. Described by surrealism founder André Breton as 'the most surrealist of us all', Miró, while influenced by both, remained independent of both Dadaism and Surrealism. Based in Paris from 1919 to 1941 and in Majorca thereafter, Miró's work has been described as psychic automatism and as a free-form expression of the subconscious. Certainly Freud is present in his phallic 1983 *Dona i Ocell* (Woman and Bird), an immense polychrome ceramic-covered cylindrical column in Barcelona's Parc de Joan Miró. He donated many of his works to the city through his Foundation (*see p. 129*).

Modernisme Catalonia, ripe with industrial riches and renewed nationalist exuberance in the late 19th century, embraced Art Nouveau as nowhere else in Europe and created its own branch of the movement: *Modernisme*. Characterised by organic shapes and vegetable decorative elements, Art Nouveau was present in every detail of turn-of-the-century bourgeois Barcelona from cribs and Christening gowns to beer mugs, churches, chapels, and tombstones. Architecture was by far the crowning strength of *Modernisme*, whose masters were Lluís Domènech i Muntaner, Josep Puig i Cadafalch and Antoni Gaudí. *Modernista* painters included Santiago Rusiñol and Ramon Casas.

Mudéjar Moorish taste and workmanship used in the construction of Romanesque, Gothic and Renaissance buildings in Christian Spain. Considered Spain's most distinctive and defining architectural style, the Mudéjar is characterised by elements of Islamic art and ornamentation such as exposed brickwork, horseshoe arches, tilework and wood and plaster carving. Neo-Mudéjar elements are found in Gaudí's Casa Vicens (*see p. 109*), and Park Güell (*see p. 112*), with the use of *trencadís*, broken bits of polychrome tile on curving surfaces.

Neoclassicism The Neoclassical austerity of the 18th century, theoretically rooted in classical antiquity but in practice a relentless exercise in monotony and uniformity, hit Barcelona just as the city walls along the Rambla were coming down. Hence the Neoclassical squares of Sant Josep (now La Boqueria; *see p. 28*) and Plaça Reial (*see p. 62*).

Nonell, Isidre (Isidre Nonell i Monturiol; 1876–1911) Charismatic post-*Modernista* painter. When Nonell exhibited at the Sala Parés gallery (*see p. 72*), critics described him as Impressionist in style. He became increasingly interested in society's outcasts and produced a number of paintings of gypsies, which can be viewed at the Museu Nacional d'Art de Catalunya (*see p. 126*). His work, which slowly became more Expressionist, shocked and disturbed Barcelona sensibilities at the time.

Noucentisme After Catalonia's *Modernisme* frenzy began to abate, *Noucentisme* (derived from *nou* - new - and *nou cents* - nine hundred- as in the year 1900) was a reaction to the ornamental profusion of Art Nouveau and a return to more orderly lines and surfaces.

Olot School Landscape painters of the mid-19th century. Originating as a School of Drawing in 1783 at Garrotxa in the province of Girona, it was not until Joaquim Vayreda, the founder, rose to fame that the Olot School became a recognised landscapist group. The Olot School included painting, sculpture, ceramics and nativity scenes (*pessebres*). Well represented in the Museu Nacional d'Art de Catalunya's Modern Art collection (*see p. 128*), leading painters include Vayreda and his disciple Josep Berga Boix.

Picasso, Pablo Ruiz (1881–1973) Co-founder of Cubism and the 20th century's most famous painter, Picasso studied and worked in Barcelona, off and on between the ages of 15 and 23 while his father taught at La Llotja art academy (*see box on p. 81*).

Plateresque Intricate decoration, unique to 16th century Spain, in the style of silversmith work, taking elements from Renaissance, Moorish and Gothic design. Puig i Cadafalch employed a neo-Plateresque technique on two of his commissions in the Eixample district: the window decoration of Casa de les Punxes (*see p. 109*), and on the façade of Palau Baró de Quadras (Casa Àsia; *see p. 111*).

Puig i Cadafalch, Josep (1867–1956) Architect, scholar, writer, politician and statesman, Puig i Cadafalch was the most politically active and powerful of the *Modernista* architects. His early style combined an affinity for Nordic Gothic forms with the lines and tradition of the Catalan *mas* or manor house. His most famous work in Barcelona is the Casa Amatller (*see p. 105*), influenced by Flemish architecture. In the Casa de les Punxes (*see p. 109*) Puig i Cadafalch realised his most extravagant Nordic Gothic fantasy. An expert on medieval Catalan art and architecture, Puig i Cadafalch authored important studies on these subjects throughout his life, and, with his teacher Lluís Domènech i Montaner, masterminded the transfer of Romanesque mural paintings from Pyrenean churches to what is now the Museu Nacional d'Art de Catalunya (*see p. 126*). He was dismissed from his post of architect to the 1929 International Exhibition by the ruling dictatorship, and under Franco he was forbidden to work as an architect in Spain. He settled in Paris, and later in Roussillon, where he continued his Romanesque studies.

Renaissance The 15th- to 17th-century European Renaissance caught Barcelona in economic decline as the Catholic Kings turned their attention to the New World colonies and wealth poured into central and southern Spain, leaving the city with a scarcity of Renaissance works. The palaces along Carrer Montcada (*map p. 49, F4*) are essentially Catalan Gothic with Renaissance touches. The Italian Renaissance-style main façade of the Generalitat de Catalunya (*see p. 60*), the Generalitat's Capella Nova (New Chapel), the Palau Centelles behind the Town Hall, and Casa de l'Ardiaca (*see p. 54*) opposite the Cathedral are Barcelona's main Renaissance structures.

Romanesque Type of architecture that prevailed throughout Europe from the mid-11th to the mid-12th century. The term Romanesque identifies the source of the architectural style in the structures of the Roman Empire. Added to classical elements were barrel vaults and abutments as basilicas and churches grew in size. Barcelona's Romanesque structures include the churches of Sant Pau del Camp (*see p. 38*) and Santa Anna (*see p. 60*), and the Capella del Marcús.

Rusiñol, Santiago (Santiago Rusiñol i Prats; 1861–1931) Playwright, short story-writer, painter and collector, who came from a well-to-do family of textile barons. Bored with the family business, he broke ranks and went to Paris, from which he returned as a leading exponent of Catalan *Modernisme* and an advocate of the 'art for art's sake' philosophy of the British Decadents. Rusiñol was a key member of the Els Quatre Gats art café group. In both his painting and his short story writing he criticised the social disparities between bourgeois and working-class Barcelona. He ignored family pleas to give up his bohemian existence, and was a frequent exhibitor at the Sala Parés art gallery (*see p. 72*). Rusiñol's best paintings, such as *Figura femenina* (1890), his study of a woman sitting beside a fireplace, study human subjects with power and a sense of complicity. His works can be seen at the Museu Nacional d'Art de Catalunya (*see p. 126*).

Sgraffito Derived from the Italian *ex-graffito*—low relief extruded from a background by carving around figures—*sgraffito* design became popular in Barcelona during the Baroque period from the mid to late 18th-century. The Gremi dels Velers (Silkweavers Guild) next to the Palau de la Música Catalana (*see p. 57*), and the Gremi dels Revenedores (Retailers' Guild) over the Roca cutlery shop (*see p. 70*) are two of Barcelona's best preserved designs, although the most beautiful examples of *sgraffito* are the ones that have almost faded away such as the Casa de les Quatre Estacions (House of the Four Seasons) just down from the Palau de la Música Catalana, at no. 18 Carrer Sant Pere Més Alt, and the Bacchic scene high on the wall halfway down Carrer de la Carabassa, at no. 17 (*map p. 49, G2*).

Subirachs, Josep Maria (b. 1927) Sculptor, designer and engraver whose lifetime project is now carrying on Gaudí's work at the Sagrada Família (*see p. 99*), currently the Passion Façade. Other Subirachs works can be seen in Plaça Catalunya (*map p. 22, B4*), where his cold and angular monument to Francesc Macià can be observed in the reflecting pool across from the top of the Rambla, and in the Barcelona Town Hall (*see p. 60*), where his hermaphroditic marble nude stands at the bottom of the right-hand stairway.

Surrealism A literary and art movement sparked by Freud's exploration of the subconscious imagination as revealed in dreams, surrealism was founded in Paris in 1924 by André Breton. Salvador Dalí and Joan Miró are Catalonia's most important Surrealists. Dalí painted dream-inspired symbols such as melting watches and giant metronomes while Miró derived colourful imagery from psychic automatism and spontaneous thought (*see Miró Foundation on p. 129*).

Trencadís Decorative technique championed by Gaudí and particularly his collaborator, Jujol, in which pieces of broken tile are assembled to produce a mosaic. Jujol's bench at Park Güell (*see p. 112*) is the best example of *trencadís* in Barcelona.

Vayreda, Joaquim (Joaquim Vayreda i Vila; 1843–1894) The founder of the Olot School (*see above*) of landscape painting. His best-known canvas is the ominous *Recança* (Sorrow), with its melancholy atmosphere of gathering dusk, black rooks flocking like vultures, and a family on the move with all its meager possessions heaped into ox carts. It can be seen in the Museu Nacional d'Art de Catalunya (*see p. 126*).

index

Numbers in italics are picture references. Numbers in bold denote major references.

art/shop/eat Barcelona
Fully rewritten second edition 2008

Published by Blue Guides Limited, a Somerset Books Company
Winchester House, Deane Gate Avenue, Taunton, Somerset TA1 2UH.
www.artshopeat.com
www.blueguides.com
© Blue Guides Limited
Blue Guide is a registered trademark

ISBN 978-1-905131-24-2

Editor: Sophie Livall

Photo editor: Hadley Kincade
Layout and design: Anikó Kuzmich, Regina Rácz
Maps: Dimap Bt
Floor plans: Imre Bába
Printed in Singapore by Tien Wah Press Pte

Photo credits: p. 151, which forms part of this copyright page

We welcome all comments, corrections and views. We want to hear all
feedback, and as a mark of gratitude we will be happy to send a free copy of
one of our books to anyone providing useable corrections, constructive
criticism, or gross flattery. Please contact us via our website,
www.artshopeat.com

SOMERSET BOOKS